Fall From Innocence

Memoirs of the Great Depression

Edited by
Guida Jackson
Jackie Pelham

Page One Publications
Houston, Texas

Fall From Innocence

Memoirs of the Great Depression

Edited by
Guida Jackson
Jackie Pelham

Copyright © 1997
Page One Publications
Individual story copyright by respective authors
and used by permission

Cover Photograph and Design
by Jackie Pelham

Library of Congress Catalog Card Number: 97-75551

Printed in the United States of America

Published by

Page One Publications
2003 Corral Drive, Houston, TX 77090
281-440-6701

ISBN 0-9627844-1-9

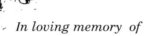

In loving memory of

Naide McDaniel
whose encouragement made this collection a reality

and

Vi Kracklauer
whose adventures inspired the project

Table of Contents

Section I Texas

Section II - Oklahoma and the South

Section III - The Midwest

Section IV The Northeast

Photographs

Preface

Our original desire was to document the literature of Texas by Texans, and we were surprised and pleased at the diversity of these Depression essays collected by Guida Jackson. This is an extraordinary book in that it contains a sampling of vast areas of the United States and abroad during our country's *Fall From Innocence*.

Over half a century has passed since the stock market crash in 1929, and much has been written by adults who weathered the devastating years that followed. However, many of the wonderful memoirs in this book were written as seen through the eyes of the young who were partially shielded from the reality of the times. Their stories are sometimes sad, but just as often, heartwarming and amusing. If there is a common thread among the lines, it is that everyone pulled together, sharing their meager possessions with the less fortunate.

The stories are grouped according to geographical location, such as Texas, Oklahoma and the South, the Midwest and the Northeast. Little editing was done in order to maintain the author's voice and the flavor of the time as he/she remembers it. A short biography of each writer is included showing that trials and tribulations are not necessarily bad things, because they make us strong, and that whatever the circumstances we can become productive and important individuals to society.

Eyewitness accounts of this fading era will eventually come to an end. We hope you enjoy reading ours.

—*Jackie Pelham*

Page One Publications

vii

Introduction

This collection was inspired several years ago by the late Vi Kracklauer at a writers' meeting in Conroe, Texas. During a discussion about Native Americans at the Hughie Call Scribblers Club, Vi surprised us newcomers by relating that she had once taught American Indian children and had lived for several years on a North Dakota reservation.

Vi told of another young woman who rode a horse bareback all the way from North Carolina to North Dakota to take a teaching job on the reservation. Imagine a young woman daring to make such a trip alone on horseback today.

It is difficult now to imagine an America where, in some areas, there simply were no jobs to be had. The phenomenon was not unknown in Ireland during the potato famine, or in parts of India, or Tsarist Russia, but America had always been the land of opportunity. There was work for anyone willing to turn a hand. By the Thirties we didn't realize the extent to which our economy was tied, not only to the stock market, but to world economy. The stock market crash of October 25-29, 1929, was felt around the world. By the last day of Herbert Hoover's term in March of 1933—presidential terms ended in March—the banking system had collapsed, and it was every man for himself. As factories closed and related jobs dried up, men *and* woman were driven to desperate lengths to feed themselves and their families. The Depression was to linger on for over twelve years.

Vi's account of the young horseback rider's courage born of desperation prompted me to wonder if there were other such experiences among the writers present, and the idea of collecting these accounts took root. Unfortunately, Vi did not live to write her own story, but her daughter Mary Kracklauer was able to reconstruct it and verify details with family and friends.

Gradually the project expanded to include people from as far away as Nacogdoches. But whereas my expectations were to receive primarily descriptions of life in East Texas, the accounts were surprisingly diverse—the locations ranging from New York to California to Florida to Spain. Such is the nature of our transient society, that not one of these writers weathered the Depression in Conroe, Texas.

Surprising, too, is the relative ease in which some of these writers passed the lean years. While a few recount wearing cardboard in their shoes, others tell of buying their first automobile during those days. However, it must be remembered that many of these writers were children or young adults at the time, endowed with the natural optimism and carefree attitudes of youth. Doubtless in many cases they were shielded from much of the anxiety felt by their elders, upon whose shoulders the gravest responsibilities rested.

Too, time dims our recollections. Most of us tend to erase unpleasantness and to focus on the good times. We share the national characteristic of optimism, but optimism has its down side. We Americans have been accused by detractors within and outside our borders of being a nation of Pollyannas. We are also frequently criticized for being blind to the lessons of history.

If there is one great gift which the Depression bestowed, it is that it was excellent preparation for the material deprivations of the war years to come. People had learned well how to do without; once the defense industry geared up and jobs were plentiful again, people must have considered the scarcity of certain consumer commodities no sacrifice at all.

If there is a negative legacy of the Depression, it is the almost unbridgeable rift of understanding between Depression survivors and baby boomers, considered the most insatiable consumers the world has ever known. It's a case of the penurious versus the prodigal, in extreme instances. Boomers, to say nothing of their offspring of Generation X, often have little comprehension of how their Depression elders came by their frugal ways, and the oldsters find the "me" generation's attitudes wasteful and short-sighted.

It is to foster more intergenerational understanding that these memoirs are offered, as well as to celebrate a few basic moral principles about helping others. In their stories, the writers also pass on valuable lessons learned about thrift, preparedness, and the pleasures of a simple life that must never be forgotten.

—*Guida Jackson*

Section I

Texas

RUBY C. TOLLIVER

The New Deal in Port Arthur, Texas

Franklin Roosevelt, touted as the hope and salvation for our nation, became president March 4, 1933. We in Port Arthur, Texas, expected miracles. Every picture show featured Roosevelt's rousing New Deal song. Here is what I recall of that song:

> *"There's a new day in view*
> *And there's gold in the blue,*
> *And there's hope in the hearts of men.*
> *From the plains to the hills,*
> *From the farms to the mills*
> *For the road is open again."*

We kids felt that prosperity was just around the corner. Our parents knew it would take a little longer.

One of the things I remember about that same time is the repealing of Prohibition. "Three-point-two" the beer was called since it contained only 3.2% alcohol.

In all of my eleven years I had never seen a bottle of beer. I knew beer existed. In fact, I knew where the local bootlegger lived and prospered. My mother did not allow me to walk on the side of the street where he lived.

Now that beer was legalized, my father felt free to add it to his menu in his cafe. The long counter in the cafe appeared very festive to me. There were bowls of free pretzels and hard boiled eggs for the thirsty drinkers. The foaming beer filling the frosted glasses tempted me.

My father finally allowed me to taste the amber drink. I almost spewed it out there at the counter. It tasted like "666" or "Three Sixes" as it was called, the patent quinine medicine we used to ward off malaria. I have not tasted beer since. The very thought makes me shudder.

Another important thing I remember of that time was the night Port Arthur turned back on the street lights. Loss of taxes and other revenue during the Great Depression had forced many harsh economic measures on our town and its employees. To my way of thinking, the darkened streets was the worst thing the city had done. No longer could we play under the corner street lights. With the darkness came fear. Too many sailors were abandoned at the docks by tied-up tanker fleets. Strangers from foreign lands wandered our streets. Seafarer and dock worker labor unions were being formed. The frustrated unemployed fought on the docks, and even downtown. Their troubles and meanness penetrated our residential areas.

After a neighbor's house was robbed and the young daughter raped, Mother nailed our window screens to the wall. She placed blocks of wood to keep our open windows from being raised over five inches in an effort to thwart intruders.

I began to have nightmares. No longer were ghost stories amusing. Stores were broken into—not by vandals, but by the hungry and dispossessed.

Finally, the city fathers decided there was money enough to turn on the street lights again. What a celebration we enjoyed that first night!

A downtown street was blocked off and Port Arthur had one of its famous street dances. Sacks of cornmeal were scattered over the pavement to help the dancers glide freely. Cajun bands vied with recordings coming over loud speakers. Throngs of people of all ages filled the street. Men and women danced. Women and women danced. Children danced. I envied them. But we were "Baptists". We were lucky our parents permitted us to watch. That night was the beginning of Port Arthur's "New Deal's Recovery" as it was called.

The Port Arthur Independent School District was one of the wealthiest school districts in the state. Most of its tax money came from the Texas Company and Gulf Refineries and their support industries. The schools were excellent, offering us many advantages. The PAISD was the first district to offer free kindergarten. Swimming pools were located in each school. Classes in woodworking, metal shop, cooking and sewing were offered from the fourth grade up. We were among the first districts to offer kindergarten plus twelve grades, instead of the eleven offered in other Texas schools at the time. Our district did not allow women teachers to marry and retain their jobs, although widowed teachers were allowed in the system. The refineries were hard hit by the Depression. Many workers were laid off. School tax collections were at an all time low. Elementary schools went on half-days. Teachers who were not laid off had to teach morning classes and then a new group in the afternoon. It was during this time when I was in the sixth grade I did something I had never done before or since. I played hooky with a girl friend. We had a miserable time. We walked over to the Pleasure Island and hid in the empty ball park. We had only our lunch money to spend, but the concession stands and the amusement park were closed. We had made no plans, and didn't know what to do. We were frightened that our all-knowing school truant officer would discover us.

To make matters worse, Miss Carter, my very favorite teacher of all time, was ill that day. Since she lived around the corner from our house, she had asked me to deliver some papers to the substitute teacher when I went to school that afternoon. Having to lie to her the next day about my absence and failure to deliver the papers to the substitute teacher was the worst punishment I could have received. I remember that later on, my young brother played hooky all the time. He would go fishing in the Texas Company reservoirs. Being a girl, I wouldn't have done that even if I had known how to fish.

One of the pleasures we enjoyed during the Depression was the tent shows that came to town. A big tent would rise on Gilliam Circle under the giant water tank. Inside the tent sawdust covered the ground. We sat on rickety folding chairs to watch the actors perform in their three-act dramas. The plays were romantic in tone and clean in language. There usually was a handsome man or a beautiful woman who would sing for us between the acts. "Among My Souvenirs" was the song we all loved and demanded of the male singer time and time again at the last tent show I attended. Before, during and after, the show's allegedly life-saving, medicinal cure-alls were hawked.

Having to live through the Great Depression in Port Arthur wasn't all bad. Our very large and up-to-date Gates Memorial Library offered escape from the bad times through reading. Most of the churches had planned activities for boys and girls. The First Baptist Church (across the street from our home) often sponsored trips to the Magnolia Park swimming pool in Beau-

(1) l-r Ruby Tolliver age 11, sister Olga and brother Jimmy - 1933

mont. City churches didn't adhere to the rural churches' belief that "mixed bathing" was sinful.

The Saturday morning picture shows that cost a dime were the highlight of each week. Boys and girls eagerly performed in the talent show that preceded the showing of a chapter of the breath-taking, hair-raising weekly serial, "The Perils of Pauline." Next came the singing of the New Deal song, followed by the main feature. If we were lucky, there would be two comedies.

During the summer months, we could, if desperate enough, go swimming off Pleasure Island pier. Between hurricanes there was a long pier built out on Sabine Lake. The water was never too deep, but the mud was. You would sink over ankle deep in the sometimes silty, sometimes gooey mud. You learned to float or swim early if you swam in the Sabine Lake.

Port Arthur had the Intracoastal Canal. On a warm sunny day you could lie on the levee and watch the ships and tugs with their barges pass by and dream of traveling around the world. The ever present breeze would stir the blossoms on the nearby oleander bushes, producing a sweet aroma that competed with the stench from the refineries.

Port Arthur was completely surrounded by smoke-puffing, ill-smelling petroleum refineries. Outside the refineries were stinky, stagnant oil pits, and swampland that smelled of dead fish and decaying marsh grass.

In spite of the hard times during the Great Depression, our family always had a beautiful Christmas tree. Daddy shared our enthusiasm for the season. He loved the time spent away from his small cafe choosing a tall Scotch pine, an Oregon fir, or a spruce. Raised on the rocky coast of Greece, he marveled at the abundance of trees in his adopted land.

These trees, symbols of Christmas, represented the "America the Beautiful" I had never seen. The crisp, pungent odors of the Christmas trees promised me there were mountains and valleys filled with towering trees, rushing streams, and sweet-smelling air.

One chilly Saturday morning my sister and I huddled on our front porch wrapped in Daddy's old army blanket, waiting impatiently for him to arrive with our promised tree. My eleven-year-old mind was filled with plans for decorating it. Jimmy, my seven-year-old brother, equally excited, ran to the corner of the

17

block every few minutes, watching for the tree-laden car. Finally, the tree arrived, and what a tree it was, perched on the top of our old car, nearly obscuring the windshield. Daddy called to us, "Come see!" as he unlashed the tree. Olga and I stared at the thing. I thought he was playing a trick on us.

"Daddy! What's—?" But Olga, who was two years older than I, apparently sensed I was about to ruin his surprise.

She grabbed my arm, and her sharp nails dug into my flesh. "Quit! You're hurting me!" I tried to loosen her grip on my arm.

"Be still," she hissed. "Maybe he didn't have any money to buy a real Christmas tree."

"But that doesn't even look like a play-like Christmas tree," I almost wailed.

"Hush. Act glad."

How could I hush? This couldn't be our tree. I hushed. I didn't want to hurt Daddy's feelings. But the tree in no way resembled our beloved, expectant, fragrant Christmas tree. Instead of long, thin green needles, the tree had leaves—broad flat leaves with stickers around the edges. I picked up a fallen leaf and sniffed. Maybe its odor would make up for its appearance.

"Olga, smell!"

"I don't smell anything."

"I know," I said mournfully. "There's nothing to smell." I began to weep silently.

"Quit it, Ruby Lee. You want Daddy to feel bad 'cause we're so poor?" I gulped a couple of times. Daddy had finally righted the tree and was lost in its branches as he held it up for our inspection.

"What is it?" yelled Jimmy, jumping up and down, grabbing at the bright red berries on the tree.

"It's a hollaly tree, the best and biggest on the lot." Daddy's heavily accented voice rang out from the branches surrounding him. He smiled at us as he moved what seemed a seven-foot-tall and seven-foot-wide holly tree into our living room. He must have thought the consternation evidenced by Olga and me was appreciative surprise. Not so. None of our friends had ever had a holly Christmas tree. This had to be a Greek custom—and Greeks we didn't want to be—only Americans, like all the other kids.

18

I don't think it bothered Jimmy at all. He was not the conformist his sisters were. As Daddy prepared the tree stand and hung the lights, Olga and I stood mutely by, eyeing that big fat bundle of holly tree. The lovely decorations we had worked on all morning lay nearby on the dining room table—decorations inspired by the thought of an ordinary American Christmas tree.

Before the afternoon was gone, we were truly martyrs. We had succeeded in hanging every ornament, but had paid the price of trying to beautify our tree. It was like trying to put earrings on a porcupine. Our tear-stained faces and the mercurochrome applied lavishly to our scratches did not represent the true Christmas spirit. We agreed not to mention our tree at church or school. This Greek tradition was making a mockery of our American living room. Worse, I could imagine Daddy bragging to his customers at the cafe about his "hollaly tree." *Perhaps*, I consoled myself, *they won't be able to understand his English*.

By Monday afternoon, Olga had adjusted to the tree. She invited her best friend, Jenny Smith (lovely American name), to see our homemade decorations. Thank goodness, I wasn't there. I had heard Jenny laugh before about foreigners and their customs. I thought if I could sit through school Tuesday and Wednesday without anyone discovering our secret, perhaps no one would come to see me before Christmas. We would take the tree down the day after Christmas instead of New Year's Day. Then my friends would never know.

My teacher seemed to notice my silence. She kept eyeing me and asked if I felt ill. I lied. "My head hurts, Miss Carter." My fellow students did not give me a chance to elaborate. I was grateful and sat and watched the excitement grow—for them—as each tried to share his or her Christmas plans with the class.

I was practically mute that last day before the holidays. Miss Carter realized her noisiest pupil had been silent most of the day. "Ruby Lee, you haven't told us about your tree, have you?"

You bet your sweet life I haven't, I thought as I dumped my notebook to the floor to hide my flushed face. I slowly retrieved the notebook, praying silently someone would interrupt.

Then Mary, sister of Jenny, the all-American Smith girl, squeaked like a mouse. "They've got a holly tree at their house.

I know. My sister saw it."

Oh, that Jenny Smith and her big-mouthed sister, Mary. Before I could think up some dire punishment for them, I noticed my teacher was smiling the sweetest smile I had ever seen.

"Do you really have a holly tree?" she asked.

As I slowly nodded, admitting the crime, she perched on the side of her desk and began reminiscing. "Oh, Ruby Lee. I love holly trees. We always had one in the church back home in East Texas. A huge one." She described in vivid detail what were some of her finest childhood memories of Christmas time in her church as they gathered around the giant holly tree.

While the other pupils sat spellbound, listening to her story, I was trying to decide if people from East Texas were true Americans. I remembered hearing someone say, "East Texans are a breed of their own." But my teacher was a blond and looked like an American. If she thought holly trees were suitable for Christmas trees, I was convinced of it, too.

Oh, how impatient I was for her to conclude her story. My heart was finally filled with Christmas joy as I waited to invite my school friends to my home to see my beautiful American holly Christmas tree.

Ruby Tolliver was born May 29, 1922 in Fort Worth, Texas and was reared in Port Arthur her first twenty-two years. She began writing in 1965 and has had eleven young adult and juvenile books published. Number twelve is due out in Spring 1998. She has worked as ESL volunteer for thirty years, is active in Christian work having been a member forty-nine years at Mims Baptist Church. She has been married fifty-three years to construction engineer B. H. Tolliver, Jr. They have three children and seven grandchildren.

ANN H. BIANCHI

When They Paved Colquitt Street

In 1928 my parents moved into the upstairs unit of a big brown brick duplex that had just been finished on Colquitt Street in Houston, Texas. This area was on the southwest edge of town. Two blocks west was a built-up gravel top road called Shepherd Drive with big ditches on each side where the crawdaddies built their tall towers. Beyond this point there was a long stretch of empty prairie where yellow wildflowers bloomed in the spring.

Mother chose the upstairs duplex so we wouldn't have people walking over our head. Besides, over the open downstairs porch we had upstairs a south-facing screen porch that could be used as a bedroom in the heat of the summer. The duplex had a living room, dining room, sunporch, two bedrooms, a bath and a kitchen with a built-in breakfast nook. It was bigger than any place we'd ever lived before. There was piped in gas for heating and a back staircase that curved around a gas hot water heater. All the modern conveniences and a step up for a young couple from poor families. The street was topped with crushed oyster shells but the city promised it would be paved within the year.

Our family consisted of Mother, Dad, me—a seven-year-old girl—and my maternal grandmother, Mrs. Ebert. In the servant's room over the garage lived our black servant, Nora, and her seven-year-old daughter Johnny Mae. She was my constant companion. Downstairs lived an undertaker, his wife Peggy and their two little boys. Mother had a little Model A Ford and Grandmother had an electric sewing machine.

When we moved to Colquitt Street Aunt Eileen and Uncle Bernard bought a new house way out west in a place called River Oaks. Grandmother and Grandfather Herod bought a house out close to them. I didn't know for years that Dad had used his capital to buy stock in a bank.

The Christmas of 1929 was a lavish dream for an eight-year-old girl. The house smelled of pine boughs and ice box cookies baking and buzzed with secret conversations. There was a big box filled with rustling white tissue paper, bright ribbons, cards and Christmas seals under Mother's bed. When Santa came he left a two-story doll house completely furnished, and a baby doll big as a real baby called Cuddles. Right after Christmas Mother took me shopping at Woolworth's to buy real baby clothes for Cuddles.

The next year Christmas seemed different. There was still the box of Christmas wrappings under Mother's bed, the holly, pine and smilax and the ice-box cookies, but there didn't seem to be as many presents under the tree. I was too young to understand a stock market crash and what it might mean. However, Mother still had memories of a childhood when she feared there wouldn't be firewood to heat the cottage she shared with her widowed mother. She was determined I would never know a fear like that. Perhaps because my parents had grown up poor they knew how to "use it up and make it do"—anyway I didn't notice many changes.

Certainly there didn't seem to be any change in the food. Mother was strong on nutrition: liver once a week, fish once a week, cod liver oil pills every day and lots of greens. I hated greens—mustard, collard, turnip, beet greens and spinach. Every Thursday night we had liver, fried until it was hard as shoe leather and served with fried onions, potatoes and liver gravy, spinach with hard-boiled eggs and gooey rice pudding for dessert. I hated that meal but I couldn't leave the table until I had cleaned my plate. Usually I sat dripping salty tears into cold spinach while Grandmother helped Nora clear the table.

"I can remember," she'd say, "when if you bought a nice round steak the butcher would throw in a liver or a good soup bone. Nowadays, people want to charge for every last thing."

I was glad they charged for the liver—at least we only had it once a week.

The first time I was conscious of the Depression was the morning Peggy, the undertaker's wife, came upstairs in tears. There was a whispered conversation with Mother. Peggy was getting a divorce. She wept and said, "If he had ever told me how bad things were I could have cut down, but I never knew!"

Peggy and her two boys moved away and later I overheard

Dad telling Mother that the Shriners were taking up a collection so her boys would have something for Christmas. After a while Uncle Bernard rented his house to some other family and he and his family moved in with Grandfather Herod. That way they could hang on to both houses. Colquitt Street still hadn't been paved.

In 1933 we got a new president called Roosevelt. He had been crippled with infantile paralysis just like cousin Bert. But the president was much worse than Bert who only limped a little when he walked. After this new president was elected the conversation at our dinner table was about the WPA and the CCC and most of all the NRA and something called the "fair price policy". Dad was worried about a rich man telling the merchants how to price their merchandise. Dad was a "rock hard Republican" and Grandmother was a "born and bred Democrat" and sometimes the discussions got pretty heated. Grandmother slapped her hand on the table and said, "If Roosevelt hadn't started the CCC camps we would have had a revolution—just like Russia." Mother tried to be the peace keeper and "pour oil on troubled waters" whatever that meant. I didn't understand all this talk but I was required to sit at the table until everyone finished eating. It was better than doing those terribly long multiplication problems in that hated Lennes tablet.

I bought my lunch in the school cafeteria and one day I came home and told Mother that the teacher had announced that there was a "morry something" on the banks. If we didn't have money for our lunch we could get a book of chits and pay the cafeteria later. Dad said, "With the banks closed, some people are caught short of cash. But, since I'm a merchant, we have to keep cash on hand, so you can pay for your lunch as usual."

I liked buying lunch at school. In the summer when I ate lunch at home, by ten o'clock in the morning the kitchen was filled with the acrid smell of greens cooking in a big pot on the back of the stove. We ate them for lunch with pot likker, corn bread and buttermilk. Bad as liver. Sometimes, when both Mother and Grandmother went to town shopping, Nora, Johnny Mae and I split a can of oily fishy sardines with lots of Saltine crackers. This was almost as good as the tamales we bought from the little Mexican man who came around with a push cart. For a nickel he opened the steamy box on his cart and fished out four tamales which he piled on a fold of newspaper. Oh, but they were good—hot, with juice leaking out of the corn shucks. Mother believed (no doubt with good reason) that they were unsanitary and she told me they were made of ground up puppy dog tails. This was to discourage me from eating them, but it didn't. I still sneaked around to buy them.

We ate breakfast and lunch in that tiny breakfast nook, but dinner was served in the dining room. The table was set with a tablecloth and a centerpiece in the middle. In the spring we made a special trip to pick bluebonnets to put in a special hand-painted bowl for the centerpiece. Later Mother and Nora made the centerpiece of fragrant honeysuckle from the vine that shaded the front porch and frothy Queen Anne's lace that grew in the ditches. When there wasn't anything else Nora made charcoal flowers by soaking pieces of charcoal in her secret solution (vinegar and salt?). In a few days the charcoal grew white crystals all over and these we tinted pink and green with food coloring. That became the centerpiece. This was called "keeping up our standards".

Although we considered ourselves city people, we still lived like folks in a small town. Every summer we made at least one trip to the Farmer's Market down on Buffalo Bayou to shop for fresh produce. I loved running barefoot up and down the smooth cool concrete aisles while Mother and Grandmother shopped. We came home with jars of honey, fresh corn, pails of figs and a peck basket of peaches. The fruits were made into preserves, which we traded with Grandmother Herod for her bread and butter pickles and sweet relish.

This was the time of Prohibition so Mother made our own beer. The big ceramic crock was filled and placed behind the kitchen door. A clean cuptowel was placed over the top to keep out any stray flies and we waited for the beer to "work". The kitchen filled with a sweet yeasty smell as the brown liquid covered itself with a dirty cream scum. This was skimmed off every morning and Mother would taste a teaspoonful to see if the beer was ready. When that magic moment came the brown beer bottles were dragged out of the bottom cupboard. A lot of washing and sterilizing of bottles followed, because if your bottle wasn't absolutely clean the beer would blow it up. That night we began the family affair of bottling the beer. My job was to suck

24

the siphon to get the flow started between each bottle. Mother filled the bottles and Dad worked the capper. Grandmother wiped any drips off each bottle. It was so much fun even if I didn't like the taste of the green beer. The duplex didn't have too much storage space so Dad put the bottles of beer on the top shelf of Mother's closet. She checked every day of the first week to make sure the beer didn't pop the tops off the bottles and drip on the clothes hanging below.

One day Dad came home and announced that the landlord had lowered the rent again. That was strange. I was almost twelve by then and I knew that landlords went *up* on the rent. In explanation Dad said, "He said we kept the place up and he would rather have someone living here than have it stand vacant." The city said there wasn't any money now to pave Colquitt Street.

Dad had to wear a coat and tie to work, but in the hot summer time the ladies mostly wore pastel seersucker house coats until they bathed and dressed for the afternoon. I wore seersucker playsuits Grandmother made for me. She made most of my clothes for you could get cotton plaids and ginghams for ten to fifteen cents a yard. In August the whirr of her sewing machine was almost constant for she made my school dresses. She cut the cloth so close that from the yardage for a dress she also got a pair of bloomers. So if I kicked up my heels at recess my underwear wouldn't show. When Grandmother made a set for me she helped Nora make a set for Johnny Mae. The dresses were made with deep hems and growth tucks inside the waist, so they could be let out the second year, when any wear lines were carefully covered with rickrack. Mother and Grandmother took pride in taking care of our clothes. Weak spots in socks were darned before the hole wore through and they were dried on a line in the garage so the sun wouldn't fade them. Twice a month Mother's underwear was tinted with Tintex. Shoes were checked regularly to see that the heels weren't run over.

Grandmother made her own flowered percale house dresses. From the scraps she made her sunbonnets, with a crown that buttoned so it could be unbuttoned and lie flat for ironing. Every year or so the Spencer lady came to measure Grandmother for a new corset—an amazing contraption of pink cloth, whale bone stays, hooks and eyes and lacings. Grandmother had her old

25

corset (carefully mended), her good corset, and her *new* corset. She wore the old one when she worked in the yard. I never figured out how she managed to build trellises and chicken coops and weed flower beds trussed up in that corset but she did.

For her good dresses Mother used Mrs. Hamilton, the dressmaker, because Grandmother sewed to the pattern and the dresses she made didn't always fit right. One time I heard her say to Mother, "Blanche, if you'd wear a proper corset instead of the flimsy thing you call a girdle, then, if your garment didn't fit you could simply adjust your corset and it would!"

Newspapers were an important part of our life. Houston had a morning paper and two evening papers and we eagerly awaited the thump on the front porch that signaled their arrival. Sunday papers were the best. They had a big section of funny papers (we never called them comics) and they were in color. As soon as Dad was through with them, Grandmother read them aloud to Nora, Johnny Mae and me. But she read straight through. There was no skipping around to read the favorites first. This probably had more to do with my learning to read than anything else. Just to be able to read the "Katzenjammer Kids" first, before "Maggie and Jiggs".

Nora knew her alphabet and her numbers up to ten, but she couldn't read. Grandmother said, "Of course you can learn to read, Nora, *you're* an intelligent woman." So with the funny papers, the Boston School Cook Book and "sounding it out" she taught Nora to read.

It was after this that I walked into the kitchen and was surprised to find Mother and Nora hugging and weeping on each other's shoulder. It seemed Mother had tried to persuade Nora to leave and get a better job.

"You were just an ignorant girl straight from the fields when you came here, but you're well trained now, Nora. You can clean and cook and serve the table as nicely as anyone. I could get you a good place with rich people and you'd make a lot more than we can afford to pay you, now in this Depression."

Nora refused to go. "I know, Mrs. Herod, that as long as you've got a pot of beans, me and Johnny Mae will have our share."

Mother didn't bother anymore to call the city about paving Colquitt Street.

Most little girls had paper doll books filled with little girl paperdolls and suitable dresses to fit them. Sometimes the paper dolls were of Eskimos or American Indians, but never of grown-up ladies. The Houston Press ran a comic strip called "Boots and her Buddies" and Boots was a grown-up lady with curves and curls and "her buddies" were young men. One week the Press ran a paper doll of Boots in her bathing suit, with two complete outfits to dress her in. This was an immediate sensation with the paper doll set. We begged copies of the Press from all the neighbors and collected as many "Boots" as we could. We traced around her and drew additions to her wardrobe on any scrap of paper we could find and colored them with the stubs of the crayons left over from our school supplies. Boots was our Barbie Doll, but the Press didn't provide her with a Ken. I spent a lot of time pouring over old Sears and Roebucks catalogues looking for a "buddy" for my Boots. But in all the photos advertising men's suits the models were posed overlapping one another, so that at the best, Boot's buddy would be missing a foot and sometimes even an arm. Mother said you just have to imagine some things.

Grandmother pieced quilts from the scraps from all those cotton dresses and Nora and I learned to use the sewing machine piecing quilts. I wasn't allowed to cut the pieces because my corners weren't square. So I had a cedar cigar box full of quilt pieces ready to sew and a second box full of paper dolls.

Since Dad worked in his uncles' furniture store, we were able to have a radio. It was an important source of recreation, second only to the newspapers. Grandmother and Nora had their program "Betty and Bob". Mother said, "I might get interested in that program if anything good ever happened to those people, but it's just one long tale of grief." During the day the radio station played records and there was a new crooner I liked called Bing Crosby. In the evenings we had "Amos and Andy" and the "Lucky Strike Hit Parade."

About once a month we would all squeeze into the Hootenanny and take a drive. Sometimes we went to the new cemetery called Forest Lawn. Dad said it was going to be a park just like the one in Hollywood where they buried the movie stars. But it was all muddy and the water in the lake looked like ditch water and there weren't any tables and benches, so we didn't take a picnic lunch. Hermann Park was lots better.

On other Sundays Dad would drive us way out to the edge of town where there was an airport with two hangars. It was pretty with red wind socks dancing against the blue sky. We'd park and watch the pilot rev up the engine of the plane and roar into the sky. A little later you could hear the plane returning and it bounced down on the sandy runway as it sputtered to a stop. One Sunday afternoon something very exciting happened. There was a pilot who was selling rides. Mother and Dad took a ride and then they bought one for Grandmother and me. One of my most vivid memories is how the ground looked from up in the plane. The tiny streets and buildings looked like one of those boards for electric trains you saw at Christmas time, and the little bitty cars looked like bugs! After a while even I noticed that we were certainly getting our money's worth; he was giving us a nice long ride. When we finally landed we discovered that the plane's landing gear had stuck and all that time the pilot had been struggling to free it. Dad was the only one of us who knew what a landing gear was. He didn't say anything so we weren't frightened. It was just an adventure to tell our friends.

Dad was a Shriner and once a week the Shriners went to the parking lot of the big Henke and Pillot market on Tuam Street to practice drilling for the drill team and sometimes I got to go. It was lovely to race around with other kids in the cool of an evening scented with the magnolias that grew in that part of town. The air vibrated with the cadence of their steps and the shrill piping of the whistles as the Shriners wheeled and turned and marched again. At last the call, "Fall out!" Shortly the headlights of the cars blinked on and fathers and children, sweaty and exhausted, went happily home.

He also had a weekly poker game and often they played at our house. Mother was embarrassed because Colquitt Street was all rutted and full of mud holes. She'd call the city and sometimes two big dump trucks would come and chug back and forth, spreading a new layer of shell on top of our street.

Mother and her friends read novels and new ones were passed round among the family and traded with the neighbors. Mother believed that what I could understand wouldn't hurt me and what I *couldn't* understand wouldn't hurt me either, so I filled the vast hot afternoons reading novels while the katydids droned in the bushes below. Still, Mother checked sometimes.

One summer day, Dorothy, my best friend, brought over a new book. "This is a really good one," she said. "Mother read it too and we both just loved it."

I had hardly begun the book when Mother said, "Let me see what you are reading."

She started in and she kept turning the pages and reading—and reading. I was getting tired of waiting. Finally she tucked the book under her arm and phoned Dad at the store. She said the most amazing thing!

"Don, I have come down with a bad case of summer flu and I will be in bed for the next three days."

She hadn't had the flu when she took the book from me. That was something you had in the winter time when they stuffed your nose with Vick's Salve. Still, she went to bed at ten o'clock in the morning!

Three days later Mother got up and handed me the book. "It *is* a good book. Let Grandmother read it when you're through. It's very historical."

That was when I learned about summer flu. That book was fascinating. I couldn't put it down. It was called *Gone with the Wind*.

I was growing up and some Saturday mornings I was allowed to go down town to the Kirby Theater with other young girls to see a movie. For fifteen cents you saw a movie, a newsreel, a cartoon and that week's installment of the Perils of Pauline. The movie had sound but the Pathè News and the Perils of Pauline were silent and the dialogue was printed in big white letters on the bottom of the screen. After the movie we all went to James Coney Island for lunch—two hot dogs and a root beer for thirty-five cents. The whole excursion came to fifty cents. The next week I could read about the movie stars in the movie magazines at the drug store. So that year I told my folks that what I wanted for Christmas was a real negligee, like the movie stars wore.

Then I found out how to win a ladies' watch. Dad smoked cigars and the cigar company promised a genuine ladies' watch to anyone who sent in one thousand cigar bands. So I started saving the red and gold bands. Dad helped me by collecting bands from his friends and at the store. When we had a thousand he sent them off.

"Now this will take time," he warned me. "You won't get your watch for a month, maybe two months."

The weeks went by and we had Thanksgiving dinner; Christmas was almost there. Then, one night when they thought I was fast asleep, I heard Dad whisper, "Her watch came today. We'll save it and it can be her big Christmas present."

"Oh, Don," Mother said, "she saved all those cigar bands and she'll know where it came from."

"Aw, she's forgotten all about those cigar bands by now. It'll make a great Christmas present."

Christmas morning came and there was a new nightgown and "negligee" of rayon satin, decorated with lots of lace, which Grandmother had made, and my new watch. I dressed up in my new finery and trailed down the damp sidewalk to show off to my friends—and I never let on I knew about the watch. After all, some people were poor and didn't have anything for Christmas.

It wasn't long after this that Dad came home and in a very subdued voice told Mother, "We had to let Miss Abel go. Mother and Helen cried and Uncle Bert promised her that, when things got the least bit better, she'd be the first one hired back."

I was startled to see a flash of tears in Dad's eyes.

"Don, when is this going to end?" Mother asked. Miss Abel was the head bookkeeper at the store and she'd been at the store always. Uncle John and Uncle Bert owned the store, Grandmother Herod ran the drapery department, Dad and his brothers ran the office and sold on the floor and Aunt Helen worked in the office. So now, only family worked in the store. I had liked Miss Abel because when I was at the store she'd find time to show me how to type on the typewriter. She was the only one I knew personally who lost a job during the Depression.

This must have been the low point in the Depression for my parents, but I only caught a glimpse of the desperation they were feeling. Slowly things got better. Miss Abel *was* hired back and Dad and his brother traded their interest in the furniture business for three stores of their own. Herod Bros. Furniture Co. was born. In 1935, when I was fourteen, Mother got her new house in River Oaks and I cried when we moved from Colquitt Street. It was the only world I could remember. Two months later Mother announced at the dinner table in our new dining room, "Guess what? They've paved Colquitt Street. Wouldn't you

(2) Ann Herod Bianchi

know!"

When did the Depression end? Some people say it didn't end until World War II began, but for me it ended when they paved Colquitt Street.

It's been sixty-two years since Ann Bianchi left Colquitt Street as a fourteen year old girl. She completed three years of college, married, had her husband drafted, had a baby boy, and moved to New York City when David was posted there. When he was discharged, they moved back to Houston, bought a house and had a baby girl. When David was transferred to Argentina, Ann sold the house and car, gathered the children and their possessions and sailed for Buenos Aires. She learned enough Spanish to enjoy Buenos Aires for seven years and the children graduated from the American high school there. They enjoyed traveling around South America—Rio, Lima, Santiago, Bariloche, La Paz. When their youngest graduated from high school they were immediately transferred to Nigeria, set up housekeeping in Britain and the Hague, moved back to the States, built a house and survived the flood of 1994. They had seven and a half feet of water in the first floor so they lived upstairs while they gutted and rebuilt the first floor. Ann says it's been a full and entertaining life. Yesterday they got on the Internet.

THELMA VORNKAHL

Pioneers of Recycling

I was truly a "Depression baby", born in 1934 when things were probably on an uprise. My family had its own private depression: before, during and after.

My daddy was a sharecrop farmer, barely eking out a living on poor soil. However, we never went hungry. We had cattle, chickens, a vegetable garden and a fruit orchard. Canning the surplus vegetables carried us through the cold winter months in the community of Indian Creek near La Grange. Also, the men in the family provided fish, squirrels, rabbits and wild turkey.

We were pioneers of recycling. We made dresses, curtains and underwear from feed sacks; we used wax paper from cereal boxes to wrap school sandwiches: table scraps were fed to cats and dogs whose job was to hunt gophers, mice and snakes. Dishwater was slop for the hogs, which provided us with bacon, ham and other meat.

We all had chores to do when we got home from school. My older brothers and sisters dropped out of school in the eighth grade or sooner to help work in the fields of cotton, corn and other crops. The fields had to be chopped to get rid of weeds. We also picked cotton and got up at three in the morning to cut the corn tops for cattle food, definitely not a favorite pastime. We were still required to work in the fields on those days.

Although we lived way out in the country, many hungry people found their way to our door, asking to work for a meal. No one was ever turned away. Daddy brought home many hungry people, much to Mama's chagrin. One woman dropped a hot flat iron on my big toe, which is still very thick and hard. A hobo had a small child with him. Today he would be called homeless.

Mama baked bread, kolaches and rolls. When I was eight years old, I baked cakes for each birthday, including my own. I also prepared the meals for the field workers because I was a "runt" and could not do a great deal in the fields. We always tried to be the first one home from school to get the end crusts from the fresh bread. Once we cut off the sides, also. Only once.

Mama often told us to come straight home from school and not eat wild huckleberries. I remember her asking us if we had eaten huckleberries and we would shake our heads, not realizing our purple lips and teeth gave us away.

President Roosevelt created jobs for young men. My brothers worked with the CCC Camps (Civilian Conservation Corps). They helped build a swimming pool and attractive cabins at Bastrop, Texas. It is very pleasant to camp there now and see their sturdy structures. President Roosevelt also had the WPA (Works Progress Administration) for older men.

On Saturday nights, after going into town, we would have ice cream socials. My brother-in-law, his brother, son and nephew made beautiful music with guitars and fiddles; sometimes a harmonica chimed in. My favorite instrumental was "Under the Double Eagle", still a favorite today.

Many Sunday afternoons, we went to my oldest sister's home or another neighbor's, where we would have "lunch": sandwiches and cookies or cakes. We called our noon meal "dinner" and the evening meal "supper".

For entertainment, we played dominoes, pinochle and canasta. I don't know why I remember this, but once when they were enjoying popcorn, I had a very sore throat and got one of Mama's jars of canned tomatoes and ate them. Always a serious offense.

Once my older siblings and cousins were wallpapering our living room. They sang as they worked, "I'm Just Driving Nails in my Coffin", "Smoke, Smoke, Smoke that Cigarette", "Pistol Packing Mama", "You Are My Sunshine" and other period songs.

My sister four years older than I remembered hearing Mama say that she was her Depression baby. Mama told of having to go to the creek, carry ice blocks back to the house, melting it to wash her diapers.

A friend, who lived in a small community where her father was the only head of a family who had a good job, always attracted the hungry. They, too, never turned anyone away. She remembered an especially tall, handsome man who came. Her

34

mother stopped what she was doing and fixed him a meal of bacon and eggs in exchange for yard work. They remembered how hungrily he ate.

Another friend remembered her mother working in her gardens, hiring three women to cook, clean and do the laundry and ironing. She preferred working outside to doing household chores. She paid Cude, Bumsey and Sally with turnip greens and other vegetables.

They all remembered that neighbors helped neighbors and were much closer than they were before the Depression.

A former co-worker remembered that he had to hold down two paper routes in order to help his family and attend high school. His father held down three jobs to support his family of six. His wife remembered that her father lost 360 acres of rich farmland. Even though he was a large man, he wept freely.

My uncle worked in Houston as a carpenter. They lost their home. He vowed he would never buy another house until he could pay for it in cash. He finished building their large new home when the last of their five children had left home for college.

Although I have mastered part of my "Depression baby" characteristics, I am still a packrat in many ways. "These will come in handy some day," I say or "I know that I will need this tomorrow if I discard it today." I go to the other extreme when money is concerned. If I have any money left over after I pay my bills and other necessities, I get something I need or want as opposed to saving for my children or grandchildren. I agree with the bumper stickers that say, "We are spending our children's inheritance." My philosophy is "I worked hard for what I have so I will enjoy." They won't enjoy anything when they are given everything. Work never hurt anybody.

Thelma Vornkahl married at age nineteen, adopted two children, a boy and a girl, and had three grandchildren. She divorced after thirty-three years. She has tried all the crafts her friends made and finally decided her two interests are writing and reading. She presently attends meetings of Inspirational Writers Alive and is finding out how much she needs to learn! She is a survivor of four traumatic incidents—two of a personal nature: cancer resulting from chondrosarcoma, causing amputation of left leg, and a broken neck.

ELLIE MILON

A Best Christmas

There is always one special Christmas that sticks in the mind forever. For me that was 1933.

It was cold and foggy. A light rain fell and the wetness went to the bone. We were packed into my uncle's old Chevy, Daddy in front with Uncle Jimmy and Momma and my brother and I in back with all our little presents and the fudge Momma had made. The windshield wipers went thwack, thwack, and the motor grumbled.

"Are we nearly there, Jimmy?" asked Momma.

"Almost. We just passed Mr. Siros' gas station."

Mr. Siros was Grandmother's landlord. We were going to our family's Christmas Eve party at her cafe. It was called "The End O' Main Cafe" because Houston's Main Street ended there and became the highway to San Antonio. My Uncle Melbourne and Grandmother ran the cafe. Though a wonderful cook herself, she supervised an African-American woman named Sedonia who cooked from Grandmother's old southern recipes.

"Mother, do you think all the customers will be gone?" My seven-year-old stomach longed for an early serving of the family holiday meal with a main dish furnished by Grandmother.

"I don't think so," Momma said. "It's still early. What time do you suppose it is, Gibson?" she asked Daddy. No one had a watch. Her watch and Daddy's had long ago been traded off for food. The Great Depression had closed in on us like a vise. Daddy lost his job; we lost our house where we had lived only a year; we had to sell our car. We lived in Grandmother's house in the Heights along with Uncle Jimmy, and sometimes Uncle Laney, too.

"I think it's about seven," Daddy said.

Uncle Jimmy turned to the right and right again into the

driveway of the cafe. Through the misty rain the rather dim lights showed the name of the cafe. We went in through the small living quarters in the back. I could smell the chicken and dumplings right away. My stomach growled. My brother pushed me from behind.

"Hurry up, Sis. I want to put these packages on the counter."

The presents would all be piled at one end of the counter nearest the kitchen to be out of the way of the customers finishing their meals that Uncle Melbourne served up from the steam table. When the last two left, Uncle Melbourne locked the doors, turned the sign from "open" to "closed", then cleared up the counter. Momma put down the plate of fudge. Uncle Lane came in. Finally, Uncle Julian and Aunt Lucretia arrived, unwrapping our new little cousin like he was a Christmas present.

"Merry Christmas," they called. Little Julian gurgled and smiled. He had seen the Christmas tree lit up in the corner.

This Christmas was just like the one in 1931 and 1932, going to Grandmother's at the cafe. But different. Different because there was hope. The grownups were full of hope because we had a new president who was going to get things done, they said, get us out of the Depression, make jobs where there were none. They were full of stirrings of excitement that sparkled out of them and made their children feel the hope, too. A photograph of President Roosevelt hung on a wall of the cafe. There was an NRA sticker with the blue eagle in the front window. You saw those everywhere. The National Recovery Administration. We were going to recover from the bank closings and from foreclosures, the breadlines, people looking for work where there was none. Things were going to be better.

What a fine sight the presents were. All the green and red and white paper, and red and green bows. We didn't have fancy embossed gold or silver wrapping paper. Most was plain tissue paper, but to the young unjaded eyes of my brother and me the packages were beautiful. Stacks of them, all shapes and sizes. Everyone gave everyone else a gift. That's why there were so many although there were only eleven of us.

The gifts took up half the counter. Looking back, I wonder how we could afford among us to buy that many gifts. They didn't cost much, but no one had much. Maybe one cost fifteen cents, and Momma made fifteen cents for giving a finger wave. (She had gone to a beauty school to learn to do this.) Another might cost a quarter, but you could get a loaf of bread and a pound of bologna for that.

Uncle Melbourne was Santa Claus and doled out the packages, looking at the tag and calling out, "Mother, Sissy, Melbourne (my brother named after him), Gibson, Julian, Ella Mae." (That's me before they started calling me Ellie.) At last, one for me. I was so excited I tore off the paper without being careful to save it for next year. A yo-yo. Finally, another for me, a pair of wool gloves, then a wool cap. My brother got a harmonica and wool gloves and a cap, too. Next we got knee socks.

How my heart longed for toys. I knew I needed clothes, but I wanted toys to play with. I didn't watch for a package that looked like a doll. I knew Santa would bring me a Patsy doll because Mrs. Van Arsdale down the street always told Momma I looked like a Patsy doll. Santa knew I wanted one so badly since I had no doll at all anymore. Not since my brother broke the China head of my one baby doll and threw the body on the roof of the house.

Everyone was talking and laughing and thanking one another. The pile of gifts got smaller and smaller. I had a new pink teddy, another pair of knee socks, some handkerchiefs, a scarf, and a box of chocolate-covered cherries. There was one gift left on the counter, square and middle-sized, wrapped in plain white tissue paper and tied with a skinny red ribbon. I held my breath. Uncle Melbourne picked it up.

"Wonder who this is for?" he said. He looked at the tag. "It's hard to read. Let's see. Oh, yes, it's for Ella Mae." My uncles loved to tease me. He handed it to me, smiling. "It's from your grandmother."

I forgot to be careful with that paper, too. Oh, how big my eyes must have looked. It was a China tea set for four—cups, saucers, plates, and a sugar bowl and cream pitcher. Each piece was white in the center with an amber colored band around the outside and a little black dog sitting with a ball in front of him. My very first tea set.

I threw my arms around Grandmother. "Oh, thank you, Grandmother. How did you know I wanted a tea set?" She just smiled and hugged me. It was just a cheap little tea set made in

Japan in the days when that meant "jim-crack." But, to me it was like fine Dresden.

Because of the tea set, because of the shared love, the warmth inside on a cold Christmas Eve, the lights of the cafe shining alone on a darkened, deserted street, the sacrifice each adult had made to buy little gifts when there was so little money, my heart remembers that best Christmas.

Since the Depression years, Ellie Milon attended college where she majored in journalism, married twice, had three children and three or four lives. Her first husband was an army officer, so she lived at various army posts in the United States and in Germany as an army wife and mother. With her second husband, who was a musician, she ran his orchestra agency, secured all bookings, and went on all "gigs" as band manager. After an auto accident her husband had to give up the music business and they ran a direct sales organization, later turning to the breeding and showing of Shetland Sheepdogs and Irish terriers. Now widowed, she devotes her time to writing, which started out with ad and brochure copy and press releases for the music agency, segued into articles on dogs, then books on dogs and finally for the past five years, fiction.

DAVID BIANCHI

There Are No Bread Lines Here

The snooty lady in the dry goods store said Victoria was a charming sleepy little town. Well, Victoria, Texas was a small town, very old and remote, but it was not sleepy. I stood in De Leon Plaza and listened to the dusty trucks from the oil fields rattling over the old iron bridge to join the cars on Main Street; behind me a strident whistle announced another cattle train steaming north; across the street the city clock on the County Court House bonged four times; at 5:00 p.m. the oil company would burn off the useless natural gas and the whole sky would light up with red flares. In 1929 this town was not sleepy; it was my whole world and I loved it. I was ten.

When there was a break in the traffic I darted across Main Street and started home. I'd gone two blocks before I remembered Mother had told me to stop by Buckert's Butcher Shop and pick up a ten-cent round veal steak for supper. I felt in my pocket; the money was still there.

The muscles in Mr. Buckert's arms were thin and stringy but he was strong enough to wrestle a whole side of beef out of his cooler, so his apron was usually smeared with blood. When he handed me my steak, he said, "That'll be ten cents, and I threw in a little package of scraps for your new pet alligator."

I could hardly wait to get home and see him. Dad had brought him home, all twelve inches of him, in a box and when I grabbed him he was so squirmy, he almost twisted out of my hands. We had dug a foot-deep pit for him behind the wash house, and put a piece of hog wire over the top.

My dad was a railroad engineer and my town was the railroad hub for the Victoria Division. This was where the line from Houston to the Rio Grande Valley crossed the line from San Antonio to Port Lavaca, so there was a big round house where the steam engines were turned around as well as a Division Engineer's

41

office and station.

When the old frame Denver Hotel was to be replaced with a large new brick building, Dad bought the old hotel and had it taken apart, piece by piece by piece—windows, doors, shutters—all of it.

He had it moved to our lot on the corner of Wheeler and Forrest and the carpenter, Mr. Urban, reconstructed the building, with a few changes inside. It was painted tan with a dark brown trim and I lived there with my parents and my brother, Jack, who was four years older than I. Dad was a trim medium tall guy with black hair and grey eyes that could almost see into your brain. Mom was pretty with blue eyes and long brown hair she wore in two braids curled over her ears. Jack was sort of skinny and—well, he was my brother.

Recently a gas company had laid a natural gas line to the residences and Dad had piped the gas into the house, so now we had gas stoves in most of the rooms. It was a lot cleaner than our old wood stoves, for we didn't have to haul the ashes out. We also got a gas water heater that hung on the kitchen wall and was connected to some pipes that ran from the wood stove. When you needed hot water you lit it with a match and turned it off when you were through.

We only used the stoves in the winter because most of the time it was hot in South Texas. The iceman came every day and Mother had a sign with a pointer on it to set in the window so he would know how much ice to leave. In the kitchen we had a large golden oak ice box with a gallon bottle on top; a copper tube ran from the bottle under the shelf where the ice sat, to a faucet in the middle of the front of the box. When you got hot you could always dash in, grab a tin cup off the shelf and get a drink of cold water.

When our house was built Dad had planted fruit trees: so now we had all the plums, peaches and pears we could eat. Mother was always preserving. Dad had planted pecan nuts and they made shoots, but Uncle Kite Fossati had purchased an especially fine pecan tree, so Dad took cuttings from that tree and grafted them to our shoots and now they were starting to bear. Dad had a deft hand for grafting and budding—and other things too. He had a metal shoe last and could replace the worn heel on a shoe or glue on a new composition sole. He was a calm, quiet man who didn't say much, but when he did, you'd better listen. Mother was a real go-er, busy with something all the time. In the fall of 1929 something bad happened up East. A stock market crashed and a lot of people lost their money. Some people even lost their jobs. We read all about it in the paper and I asked Dad if he was going to lose his job.

He drew on his pipe and said, "No son, this family is going to be all right."

Then I read about people standing in line to get bread and I thought about Aunt Ida. She baked with a yeast "starter" my great grandmother had brought over from Germany and she made bread almost every day. I went over to ask if she was going to bake some bread for the people in the bread line.

Little and wiry, she was measuring flour into her big bowl with just her hands. Mother used a cup. She stopped and turned an intent gaze on me. "What bread line? There is no bread line here." With disapproving clicks of her tongue she held up her scolding finger. "The ideas you get David—too many movies."

I should have known; our Lutheran Church was only around the corner from our house, and if there were any bread lines or soup kitchens Mother and "the girls" would have been over at the church kitchen helping out.

Ida was one of "the girls", Mother's four older sisters. Beside Ida, there were Lula, Adele and Mae who was an invalid. There was no hospital in Victoria so "the girls" ran the Victoria Clinic. When someone was sick and couldn't be cared for at home, they were brought to the clinic and Lula, a tall solemn woman, did the nursing while Ida cooked. They both wore their hair long and coiled on top of their heads in big buns. Adele had cut her hair and had a permanent wave and looked more modern. She worked in the bank and her wages supplemented the cash from the clinic.

When Ida got a gas cook stove she kept her old wood stove in the kitchen; said she couldn't bake in a gas oven. Almost every day she made bread and *kuchen*, a type of cinnamon roll. And the sweet spicy smells in her kitchen could twist a boy's stomach into a knot. Right now my mouth was watering and my stomach gurgled.

She said, "*Hier Bubi*," and set out a plate of *leipte* cake. "The girls" spoke German among themselves, but after we started

(3) David Bianchi

(4) David Bianchi

44

school they were careful not to speak it to Jack and me. They wanted us to be all American. When Ida died, the old yeast starter died with her and I have never eaten cinnamon rolls like those again.

In the "L" between the clinic and its store house was a big old fig tree, low and open. A small boy could climb clear to the top among the big green leaves. The tree was a heavy bearer and Lula paid me twenty-five cents a pail to pick the figs. When there were more figs than we could eat or preserve, Lula sold them to a lady who ran a boarding house. Without my knowledge she put this money away for me—for when I was more responsible. When she died we found, tucked into her Bible, an envelope labeled "David's fig picking money"—two old-style big five dollar bills.

We didn't have a car but our house was only four blocks from the square. Miller's grocery was a block-and-a-half in one direction, Bettin's was two blocks the other way. Our neighbor across the street grazed her Jersey cow in the ditches alongside our street and we got our milk from her. A man with a horse and wagon delivered fresh fruits and vegetables to the door.

There's a certain amount of fame in being the only kid in Mitchell School with a pet alligator. We called him Ally and boys came to our house just to see him. At night I took a flashlight out and showed them how his eyes glowed red in the dark. But it didn't last. He just ate and grew and we had to keep digging the pit deeper. It's a tiresome thing taking care of an old alligator. But it all worked out the day Ally somehow climbed out of his pit and frightened the daylights out of our washer woman.

"I'm not coming back in this yard until that animal is gone," she said. And left the dish towels boiling in the wash pot.

So Dad had to take Ally out on the prairie and shoot him.

With Ally gone I had more time, so I went over to visit my Uncle Joe Bianchi. Cowboys and ranchers from all over Texas and Oklahoma ordered the spurs he made. He was a blacksmith and his shop was always busy with horses to shoe, plow blades to mend and wagon wheels and springs to repair. But best of all I liked to watch him take a steel bar and start a spur.

"Okay, David, crank up the blower!" he would say.

I'd dart back through the gloom and coal dust and turn the crank and the old blower would whine and the fire in the forge would crackle. Sparks flew and that steel bar would turn white hot. Then Uncle Joe would beat it into a spur—all one piece—no joints. The cowboys liked them because he put a special hook on them to open beer bottles.

That fall I was in the seventh grade, the last year of Mitchell Grammar School. Next year I'd be in high school. We read about the Depression in school but it didn't make any difference to us. Dad said there was work for anyone who wanted to work and besides my folks believed in making do and using things up. Mother darned our socks and my overalls were passed down from Jack, but it had always been that way. Things were just the same except that Mother had a baby—it was a little girl and they named her Bess. She was little and couldn't do anything and I was busy with my stuff, so I didn't see her much.

Our big excitement that year was we got a car! Mr. Atzenhofer, the Chevrolet dealer, came driving up to our house in a dark blue Chevy sedan with a little trunk stuck on the back—and it was ours! I was giddy with the excitement. Out on the Bischoff farm, where my cousins lived, they had an old Model-T that I had been allowed to drive around the prairie, but this car had a six-cylinder engine and two spare wheels built into wheelwells on each side in front of the front doors. A heat gauge for the radiator sat on the top of the hood. The wheels had wire spokes and there were rollup windows—a real sedan, not just a touring car. It cost about five hundred dollars and of course Dad paid cash for it. My folks didn't buy on credit.

No one had thought of drivers' licenses in 1931 so there was no test to take. If your legs were long enough to reach the pedals you could drive and Jack and I were both getting long legged. I don't remember if Mother took some driving lessons—I didn't. We all learned to drive except Dad. He couldn't get the hang of steering. Up in his engine he controlled the throttle and the brakes but the tracks did the steering and to him that was the way it ought to be. So Mother did all the driving and she never took the keys out of the car when she parked. Why would she? Everyone knew it was our car.

On Saturdays the country folks drove their horses and buggies into town: the men in big-brimmed hats and low-heeled "roper" boots and some of the older ladies still wearing percale sun bonnets, freshly starched and ironed for the occasion. They did their shopping and always stopped at the drug store for some ice cream before they left, or if a family didn't live too far out, they bought a big block of ice and took it back to their farm to make ice cream that afternoon. It was a big treat for folks who didn't see ice from one Saturday to the next.

Those Saturdays I had a job at the A&S Levy Dry Goods store as the cash boy in the men's department. When a customer bought something I took the merchandise and their money back to the wrapper and waited until the package was wrapped. Then I picked up their change and the package and ran them back to the customer. They paid me fifty cents for eight hours and when they got busy I would write up a sale, but I didn't get a commission. My folks gave me a quarter every week for pocket money, but this was money I had earned so, at the end of the day, with fifty cents in my pocket, I'd stop sometimes at the newsstand and buy an Edgar Rice Burroughs book about Tarzan for forty-five cents.

Our first radio was an Atwater-Kent which sat on a table with the speaker off to one side. It had three dials you had to tune exactly to bring in KPRC in Houston so it was almost too much trouble to use. Then we got a dome-shaped Philco with only one dial to tune in a station and sometimes at night we could get Saint Louis or even Chicago. One of Jack's friends was interested in radios and he helped me build a little radio for my bedroom. It was a crude thing but it worked. I got an old alarm clock, removed the bell and rigged the clock to turn off my little green Emerson fan after I had gone to sleep listening to Hildegarde.

At that time there were pulp magazines full of stories of World War flying aces and their dogfights in Fokkers and Spads. I gobbled these down, but planes seldom flew over Victoria. One day I heard one sputtering and backfiring and saw it coming in low. It was going to crash! I jumped on my bike and raced across town, following the plane until it landed on a grassy strip in Judge Fly's field. It wasn't smashed at all. Nothing in the magazines really told you how noisy planes were, so I walked out and had a good look at this fascinating piece of machinery—the first airplane I had ever seen up close.

At the Saturday movies that Depression was in the newsreel about all the men without jobs, living in shanty towns they called Hoovervilles. We kept hearing about it but Dad hadn't lost

47

his job and neither had anyone else's dad that I knew.

A big upright piano sat in our sitting room and Aunt Lula came over and gave Jack and me piano lessons twice a week. But as the hour ticked by I'd begin to squirm and she'd say, "Work, David, you must work to learn." All in all I enjoyed playing the piano until I learned from the other boys that was sissy— baseball was much better. Babe Ruth didn't play the piano. So I quit.

I had been double-promoted so I started high school a year early. The school was way on the east side of town and there was a program of four years of math and English, three years of Latin and science, two years of Spanish besides two years of history and a semester of civics and it wasn't any fun. The big boys wouldn't have anything to do with me because I was just a little squirt and I wasn't about to go back and play with those babies in grammar school. And I was too skinny for the football team.

So I got in the habit of going across the street to Krause's Hamburger Stand where there was a row of pinball machines. I stood there munching a burger and feeding my nickels into a machine. They went so fast—I never had enough to perfect my skill with the plunger. A thought came to me. Why not make some extra nickels? There was plaster of Paris at home. I kept back my last nickel for a model and that afternoon I got busy in the wash house and made some molds of the coin. The next afternoon I pulled out the alcohol lamp and started melting down lead and filling the molds. It worked great! In no time I had a pile of lead nickels which I stashed in my desk drawer. They were good copies. You could hardly tell the difference.

The next week I had a fine time playing the pinball machines all I wanted to—game after game. Then on Friday evening Mr. Krause came to the house to see Dad. He'd never come to our house before; a sinking feeling came over me. Something was wrong. After a while Dad and Mr. Krause went up to my room and searched my desk. There were my lead nickels in the back of the drawer! Dad put them in his pocket and he and Mr. Krause went into the sitting room and talked a long time while I hung around in the kitchen. I was getting awfully nervous. Maybe I should run away—where would I go? Finally Dad gave Mr. Krause some money and he left.

Dad called me into the dining room. His face was very stern.

48

"David, you have been stealing games from Mr. Krause's pin-ball machines. Those machines are part of Mr. Krause's livelihood. A way of supporting his family. You are a thief. Besides you made a duplicate of a U.S. coin, which is counterfeiting. You are a counterfeiter."

I swallowed hard. "Am I going to jail?"

"Mr. Krause is not going to report you this time. I gave him my good word that this would never happen again and you see that it doesn't." Dad began to light his pipe.

In the kitchen I could hear Mother slamming pots into the cupboard. I heard her mutter, "Metal working shop. I wonder if they know what they're teaching these boys."

I was ashamed to go into Mr. Krause's shop anymore so I had to walk two blocks over to buy lunch. My pin-ball games were over.

In 1933 we got a new president, Franklin Delano Roosevelt, and he promised to end that Depression they were having up East. He'd had infantile paralysis and his legs were in braces but everyone seemed to think he'd be good for the country. He talked on the radio in something he called a fireside chat and I listened on our Philco. He sounded friendly enough. The first thing he did was to give the banks something he called a "moratorium" and Aunt Adele got a week off from the bank.

Signs with a blue eagle and NRA began to show up in the windows along Main Street. The letters stood for a National Recovery Act which President Roosevelt said would get the country back on its feet.

In 1933 Dad traded the navy blue Chevy for a new light blue one. Jack and I always maintained the cars—patched the inner tubes when they had a puncture, changed the oil and slid underneath with a grease gun to grease the leaf springs and all the fittings. It was a dirty hands-on experience and you had to be careful; if you squeezed out too much grease from the gun you could get it right in the eye or in your mouth.

That year the President said he would feed the hungry and we did have one man, who said he was hungry, come by the house. Mother fixed him a plate of food, but she said he was just a hobo. It had become a world-wide Depression and in other countries people were hungry too. In Germany things were so bad they elected a dictator. His name was Adolph Hitler.

Victoria had two movie houses with Saturday matinees for kids. For a nickel we got a western, a serial cliff hanger, then a comedy like the Keystone Cops or Our Gang Kids and a Movietone or Pathè newsreel. Wilbur was working as projectionist at the Victoria Theater and he took me up to his booth and taught me the ropes, and pretty soon I had a job as assistant projectionist. It was mostly on Saturdays because Wilbur, with his black curly hair and big brown eyes, was popular with girls and often had a date. In the summer it was hot in the theater and even hotter in the projection booth. The only light was from the arc lights in the projector and sometimes we'd lose the arc and then the lights went out.

"Turn it on! Turn it on!" the crowd would shout. They'd start stamping in time to the chant. Up in the dark projector booth we were working with sweating hands trying to get the darn arc light going again. Or the film would break. Most of the film for the comedies and the cliff hangers was old, old, old and had been patched together again and again. Every time you made a joint you had to cut off a little of the old torn film so eventually there were big gaps in the action. In the "Perils of Pauline" one moment she was safe in the car and the next she was tied to the railroad track with a train bearing down on her. It didn't seem to matter how jerky the story was as long as we kept that film rolling.

Across the street from our house the McDonalds had an old lawn tennis court. If we kept the lawn mowed we could use it. There were no court lines and the net sagged but Aunt Adele lent me her racquet and I picked up games with the McDonald girls and anybody else who had a racquet. Then Wilbur and I started to play on the courts next to the District Engineer's office up by the railroad station. When our game got better I got a new racket—a Spalding Top Flite. Then we played on the courts at high school and in time I made the tennis team and played in the district competition. I was also on the debate team with Billy Murphy and we went to the regional competition in Kingsville. Some of the families down there put us up and we had a good time. I lost my tennis match but Billy and I won in debate.

A few weeks later Wilbur quit high school and went to work full time, so I started picking up games with Jack and his friends who gave me tips on technique. In June of 1935 I graduated high school as Salutatorian. I was sixteen. The faculty chose me as the best all-around boy student and I got my name on a plaque that hung in the school hall by the principal's office. I was the first boy to have this honor who was not a football player.

I had always figured that when I graduated from high school I'd go to work for the railroad like Dad. Start building up my seniority. But the railroad wouldn't take me until I was eighteen. Luckily Victoria had a good junior college on the same block as the high school so it was decided I should continue to go to school.

I was dating girls by then and there was this fellow in junior college called Bumpy Stone who lived down in San Benito in the Valley. He was always bragging about the good looking girls they had down there and suggested we go there one weekend.

Of course, I was always interested in meeting girls, so we left on a Friday morning. We caught a good ride with a truck driver and got into San Benito that afternoon. I was not that impressed with the girls and by Sunday we had spent all our money, so we started hitching a ride home. We did all right until we got to Alice, about a hundred miles from Victoria, and we just couldn't catch a ride with anybody. A neighbor of ours from the oil field noticed us standing by the side of the road.

"I need to get my wife's car back to Victoria," the roughneck said. "You could drive it back for me, but you'd have to fill it up with gas."

Dark thunderheads were rolling up in the west and the air had that funny metallic smell it gets before a storm. At seventeen cents a gallon Bumpy and I together didn't have enough money left to buy a whole tank of gas. A big fat rain drop fell on my head.

We got in the car and pulled it into the filling station, where I asked the attendant for a blank check, trying to be real nonchalant about it. When he produced a check I scratched out Alice State Bank, wrote in Victoria Bank and Trust, filled it out for four dollars and signed Dad's name to it. We filled the car up and headed for Victoria.

It was a sweet little Ford and we were barreling along. I saw some headlights in the left hand lane coming on fast when out of nowhere, right in front of us there was a horse drawn hay wagon with no lights going practically no miles an hour! I pulled hard right, swinging the Ford onto the shoulder, all the time praying there was no concrete culvert just ahead. We made it—but I didn't feel like singing anymore.

The first thing I did the next morning was tell Dad about that check. I didn't want him to hear about it from Aunt Adele at the bank! All the same I'd never seen Dad so mad. He sat me down in a chair and looking down, straight into my eyes, started talking in a low voice.

"David," he said. "I worked hard for my money and you, my son, have stolen from me. You took money that I had earned without asking me about it. And you committed forgery." He turned and sat down heavy in his rocker. Then got his pipe out and started to rock a little. Counterfeiting and now forgery! I guess Dad thought I'd come to no good end.

It was a bad time. When I went over to "the girls'" I'd overhear snatches of conversations—"good Christian upbringing"—and "wild oats." I was downhearted for almost a week. But it wasn't all bad; there could have been a culvert on that shoulder. Dad didn't know that and I wasn't about to tell him.

Now that I was dating I needed to make more money. Wilbur checked groceries at the Piggly Wiggly Butt Grocery Store (every one sniggered at that name) and he got me a Saturday job as a stock boy stacking cans. The manager was Mr. Roberts, a portly man but so light on his feet he just seemed to glide around. He soon let me check out customers when we got in a rush. The price was marked on the shelf below the item but there was nothing on the can or box; you just had to remember. After I had proved I had the price list down pat, he put me on as a regular Saturday checker. But about twice a month he'd pick up a basket, saunter through the store selecting items at random, and I'd have to check that basket. Just testing me. If I got one item wrong he'd let it go, but two items and I was back to stacking cans while I studied the price list.

One of the fellows I had started playing tennis with was Freddie Ennen, and our last year in junior college, we were the tennis doubles team. We went to the State Finals and won the title and our white letter sweaters with a big red "V".

One weekend Freddie had a blind date from Houston. I bet him two bits she'd be a real dud. So we fixed up that before Freddie took this girl out to Pleasure Island, our local dance hall, he'd bring her by the bowling alley. I'd be waiting there and get a look at her. When they came in I was waiting. This girl, Ann, was sort of short and she had on this sort of filmy white dress and high heels. They fooled around, bowling a few lines, and finally she wound up in the alley next to where I was bowling. She kind of tottered up to the line and just slung the ball. You could see she didn't know a thing about bowling, but she got a spare!

"Think you're pretty smart, don't you?" I said.

She looked at me sort of cocky. "If you can do better, show me."

Well, then, I had to get a strike, and I did.

That gang went on out to Pleasure Island and after I bowled a few more lines I decided to see what they were doing out at the dance hall. She was dancing with Freddie and Billy and after a while I cut in on her. I did all my special dips and stuff but she followed pretty good. She was kinda' cute.

The next week I asked Freddie to get Ann's address from Geraldine for me, and I wrote her a real smooth letter, like something out of the New Yorker magazine.

That was the year Carl Feind and Ralph Kies moved to town. Carl could play tennis and we played every chance we got, but Ralph could play the piano and he was really good. Any time there was a piano Ralph would play and everybody would gather around. Now it seemed a lot better to be able to play a piano than it had when I was little, so I went around to see Aunt Lula and tried to talk her into teaching me again.

"You had your chance, David. Now you will have to teach yourself," she said.

I was still checking groceries over at the Piggly Wiggly Butt market on Saturdays and had some money, so I went over to Hauschild's Music Store and ordered some sheet music of the new pieces: "Deep Purple", "Sunrise Serenade" and "September Song". They cost sixty cents each, but what the heck! Then all it took was practice. Ralph would help me sometimes. He was a natural; he could read music but most of the time he played by ear. Sometimes we'd meet on the second floor of the music store where they stored the extra pianos and we'd play duets.

On top of the Depression, they were having a terrible drought in Oklahoma and Kansas, and that new Life magazine was full of pictures of black clouds of dust burying whole farms and their houses. I didn't know much about the stock market but I knew about drought. We had it every summer. Sometimes the earth would bake so hard that cracks would open in the ground—and not fine cracks, either. These would be wide enough to lose a marble in. I lost my favorite aggie in one of those cracks. People up East were desperate, so the President started the WPA to give men work.

The city fathers had decided to pave Victoria's streets and they all had to be surveyed first, so after I graduated from junior college in the summer of '37, I got a job on a surveying crew. The surveyor was John Harold Lowery, a big heavyset man of fifty-five or more, who always wore a hat. He hadn't always been a surveyor, for he had invested heavily in the stock market and lost it all in the Crash. Now here he was, driving a beat-up old Dodge with a backwards gear shift, and teaching me to use a transit and level. He was the first person I had met who got hurt in the Depression.

A surveying crew has three men: the surveyor who handles the transit and two chain men. I was taken on as one of the chain men, but I soon noticed that Mr. Lowery's eyesight wasn't as accurate as mine and I slowly took over the operation of the transit. It was hot work, out in the summer sun, and we were always glad when we worked up to a filling station and could stop for a drink. Just plunging your hand into the icy cooler would cool you off a little and then you pulled out that tall bottle of ice cold NeHi red soda. Gosh but it was good!

We surveyed on one day and drafted up the plats the next day in the building where the City Engineer, Mr. Miles, had his office. A tall thin man with a burr haircut, he coached us in drafting in a big room on the second floor and he checked us pretty close because he had to sign those plats as the registered engineer. Some days we had other surveying jobs that took us out into the countryside.

Mr. Miles paid me fifty cents an hour and that came to about twenty dollars a week, plus overtime, so I went down to the bank and opened a checking account.

Carl Feind and Hawes Hiatt, a new fellow we had teamed up with, found a real bargain—a Model T Ford for fifteen dollars! It was such a good buy that I went in with them and we bought it—five dollars apiece. It was kind of beat up and the top was gone, but we reworked the engine, and sanded the rust off the body and then it was ready for a paint job. We decided a light blue

Model T would look just great!

When we finished fixing it up we decided to take it on a road trip to see how it would hold up. I'd been writing to that girl, Ann Herod, in Houston so I set up a date with her. The old Model T did great on the road; our only worry was no top, but we didn't hit any rain. When we got to Houston, Carl and Hawes dated two nurses who already had a car, so I had the Model T all to myself.

At Ann's house, she and her mother both came out to look at my car. Mrs. Herod was dressed in a golden colored slack suit and had a lot of make-up on, even before lunch time. Most girls' mothers didn't look like that.

Ann asked her mother if she could go to Sylvan Beach with me, but Mrs. Herod said, "Not in that car."

My heart sank. I didn't want to spend the day just sitting around Ann's house, but what could I do?

"Wait a minute," said Mrs. Herod and went back in the house. "Here," she said when she came out. "Take my car," and handed me the keys. "Don't worry about me. I'll drive the Model T."

What could I say? I handed her the key to my car—Carl's car, Hawes' car—and crossed my fingers.

So Ann and I went to Sylvan Beach in her mother's car and had a great time. She was a pretty keen girl. And when we got back that night the Model T was parked exactly where I left it, safe and sound. I didn't believe Mrs. Herod had driven it at all. She sure was a different kind of mother.

Two days after I got back from Houston Mr. Miles called me into his office. Sitting on the corner of his desk, rolling a pencil between his fingers, he said, "David, why don't you think about going to A&M next fall? You should get your degree because you'd make a good engineer, you have a knack for it."

This was something I had never considered. Jack had a good job in Corpus now; he hadn't gone to college. I didn't know anyone in my family who had gone. How much did it cost? I talked it over with Carl and Hawes; they said they'd go if they had the money. Ralph Kies was going.

I got the information from A&M and did a lot of figuring before I went in to talk to Dad about it. I figured that by the end of the summer I'd have money saved to pay my tuition if he could pay the room and board.

Dad took the letters from the college, leaned back in his rocker and studied them. Finally he said, "I think we could afford to do that."

Hey! I was going to college! It didn't seem real. I had to buy my uniform up at College Station, but I'd need to buy some brown shoes. Nice to have some money for this emergency. I bought some Packard shoes with pointed toes and wrote a check for them.

Within weeks I was up at A&M and the first thing my upper classmen said was, "Where'd you get those pointy-toed shoes? They're going to kill your feet when you start drilling."

I was assigned to Battery D, Coast Artillery and we were bunked in Puryear Hall where there were four rooms with three bunk beds to a room and a bath at the end of the hall, on both floors. The whole corps formed up and marched to every meal and in the afternoon we drilled. Within ten days I had another emergency. The upper classmen were right; I had to buy another pair of shoes.

The upper classmen, particularly the sophomores, made it their business to make a freshman's life miserable. You always stood at attention and you ran their errands. You had to know all their names and if one of them got miffed with you he could order you to eat "at attention"—that is, sitting very straight and moving your fork "on the square". A real pain. But next year I'd have some freshmen. I could hardly wait.

A&M was a military school and when the Nazis overran Poland in March of 1939 we talked about it. It looked like there would be war in Europe but Mr. Roosevelt said that the U.S. would remain neutral. That was the summer the government began a program of rural electrification. I remembered my Bischoff cousins out on the farm at Inez, with no electric lights or fans or ice. It would be a lot better for them. An engineering firm called Beavers and Lodell hired me to draft up the field notes brought in by the REA surveyors. That fall, at the beginning of my junior year at A&M, France and Britain declared war on Germany, but our president still said we would not get entangled in foreign wars, so there didn't seem to be anything to worry about.

Ann was at Texas University now and we both kept going back and forth, usually on the bus. We would walk through the deep shadows on the A&M campus and we would walk to the dorm that was reserved on weekends, just for visiting girls. Football games—mums with maroon and white ribbons—strains of "Song of India" drifting from the windows—corps balls. It was a great time.

Spring term drifted into summer. Hawes had a job in San Antonio and we could split an apartment, so I talked Mr. Lodell into putting me in the Beavers and Lodell office there.

San Antonio was loaded with movie houses, some of them lavish. The most spectacular was the Aztec, decorated to look like Aztec temples, with lots of gilt. It had opera boxes sticking out the side walls and overhead a blue sky ceiling. When the house lights dimmed, bulbs in the ceiling came on and twinkled like little stars. The movie had a sound track, but there was still organ music for the extra features.

With a casual air the organist in an immaculate white linen suit with a black shirt would stroll in, smooth his hand over his black hair, slicked back with Vaseline Hair Tonic a la George Raft, ease onto the organ stool and hitch up his trousers at the knees to save the crease. His name was Dick Gordon and he was a nice guy when you got to know him. He had his pilot's license and spoke Spanish. All in all, a pretty sophisticated guy.

Dick not only played the organ, he repaired them. One day he invited us to fly down to Villa Acuña with him to repair an organ.

What a streak of luck! I'd never been up in a plane! I looked at Hawes. "Sure we'll go!" we chorused. "Where are we going?"

"Dr. Brinkley's place. You know, the monkey gland man."

Of course we had read about him in the papers. He was supposed to transplant monkey glands into humans and make them a lot stronger or make them live longer. He had this terrifically powerful radio station and could broadcast over half the United States. What an adventure! Dick felt he was a professional pilot and to make sure we knew it he showed up at the airport in riding pants and boots. When we had all folded our lanky bodies into the cabin of the little plane, Dick adjusted the silk scarf at his neck, studied the controls and revved up the engine. We rolled down the landing strip and then—we were up.

Dick gave the plane a ninety-degree roll, then straightened it up and we settled down to watch the brush country slide away beneath us. It seemed like no time before we were crossing the shallow, muddy Rio Grande. There was the town of Villa Acuña below like a toy village, but I didn't see any airport. The plane began to descend, we skimmed right over the roof of a Mexican hacienda, and Dick landed, running the wheels in the furrows of the plowed field behind the house.

I had never been in a foreign country before but I could have closed my eyes and still known we were in Mexico—there was that smell of a Mexican restaurant—onions, garlic and chile peppers. The house was the epitome of all haciendas—a solid white-washed wall dripping with fuchsia bougainvillea and then a tiled entrance hall. A housekeeper ushered us into a great room hung with tapestries and Mexican serapes and filled with heavily carved dark furniture. There was an enormous fireplace at one end and at the other the biggest organ I had ever seen. The pipes covered the whole wall. Dick got right to work. Hawes and I toured the house, peering out at the patio with its fountains and statues, climbing the side staircase to the balcony above the living room. It was the most magnificent house I had ever seen.

It was late afternoon when Dick finished, and it was time for the flight back through the twilight. Below us the lights of scattered towns shone and lights on cars made white and red chains on the highways. Flying was the greatest! A final decision on my college major was coming up but this flight settled it. I'd go for a degree in aeronautics.

But in 1940 Texas A&M didn't offer a degree in aeronautics, so my faculty advisor suggested that I take a degree in Mechanical Engineering with a major in aeronautics.

The days flew that senior year as I plowed through all those engineering courses and tried to see Ann at least every other weekend. Finally it was over and the job offers began to come in. By then U.S. industry was gearing up to help Britain fight the Nazis, and it seemed the Depression was almost history. The U.S. was building Hudson bombers and aeronautical engineers were in demand, so I decided to go to work for Lockheed in California for two hundred dollars a month. The only cloud on my horizon was I had to register with the Victoria Draft Board.

There was just one thing I had to have. In California you have to have a car. So, after some serious consideration, I went to see Dad.

"Why don't we go over to the Ford Agency and see what kind of a deal we can make," he said.

I was surprised. Dad pretty well let me pick out the one I wanted, so I got a green Ford convertible coupe. It cost $1,067 and at thirty dollars a month it would take three years to pay it off, so I guess Dad didn't think I was so hopeless after all.

I drove it over to Houston to show Ann. She ran her finger over the curve of the fender, got inside, inhaled the scent of the leather and said, "Wonderful. And it's a convertible!"

She was wearing my A&M senior pin by then and she had fixed it with her folks to come out to UCLA in Los Angeles, so once I kissed her good-bye it was "California, here I come!"

David Bianchi graduated from Texas A&M with a BS in Mechnical Engineering June 4 1941. Married September 1942. Worked at Lockheed Aircraft, Burbank, California until 1944, left Lockheed as Structural Design Engineer, worked on Hudson bomber, Constellation transport, P-38 fighter and P-80 fighter. Drafted into US Navy with rank of Ensign, spent time in Navy at Bureau of Aeronautics office in New York City, discharged July 1946. Managed small furniture store in Houston, Texas until 1954. Worked on drilling rig for six months. Worked for Baker Oil Tools, later Baker-Hughes in many positions, until retirement in 1986. Field Service engineer in United States for five years, seven years in Argentina as VP/GenMgr of small Argentine subsidiary, stints in Nigeria, England and Holland managing foreign subsidiaries before returning to main office in Houston. Used retirement years to practice the "three G's" - Golf, Gardening & Genealogy.

R. D. "BOBBY" JACOBS

A Depression Hurricane
in Port Arthur, Texas

My earliest memories of growing up in Port Arthur, Texas had to do with horses. We had horse-drawn ice cream wagons, ice wagons, and garbage wagons.

The traffic light downtown had a bell that rang every time the light changed. The why of that I could never figure out. Were there people driving who couldn't see the light changing or was it a warning to pedestrians to get out of the way? Anyway, the bells must have worn out by the early Forties, because they were gone by the time I returned from the Navy.

The annual Santa Claus parade was always a special event in our lives. From the time I was a small child we went early to find a good place from which to watch. Faded candy canes decorated each light pole. Faded or not, they were beautiful to me.

We always chose to stand where the parade began. Santa rode on a flatbed float, yelling "Ho! Ho! Ho!" as he threw candy to the children lining the street. One year, for some reason, we arrived late and had to take a spot in the last block of the parade route. By then, Santa wasn't yelling "Ho! Ho! Ho!" but cursing, and instead of throwing candy, he was swinging his bag with all his might and knocking the older kids off his float. Needless to say we went back to that same spot every year after that to view "the action." My mother laughed until she cried every time we went.

I remember my first movie, called a "picture show" then. I was six years old. I went with our neighbors to the Majestic Theater on Houston Avenue. It was a "silent" cowboy show accompanied by a man playing the huge organ. He provided mood music to match the action. I was hooked. But this was the year before the Big Depression. For several years, money was short and movies were out of the question.

We did have one plus—Sam Jones. He lived around the block from us with his grandparents. His mother had a good-paying job downtown and every Saturday he would visit her. She would give him money to go to the picture show. On Saturday evening, the kids in the neighborhood would meet with Sam, and he would tell us in detail, with much expression, the whole story. You've never heard so many "but before thats" or "oh, I forgot to tell you." We hung onto every word. During the following week we would "playlike" the show, sometimes with carved wooden rubberband guns.

Sam was into Frank Buck during those days. We agreed that some day we would explore Africa. The nearest we came to that was exploring the large Texaco reservoirs.

My mother's Uncle Sherb, a shade-tree inventor for the oil patch that was and is Spindletop, visited us often. On one of his trips, he made a deal with Mother to wash his shirts. He would drop them off in the wash house and pick them up later. One day when we were having a new roof put on the house, Mother noticed that Uncle Sherb had more dirty shirts than usual, but she put them to soak.

At quitting time the six men who had roofed the house were milling around the wash house. Not one of them had a shirt on. Mother, realizing what had happened, took some brown paper bags out to them. They wrung the water from the shirts and took the shirts home in the brown paper bags.

One hurricane I especially remember—the 1934 storm. Hurricanes were not named in those days, and perhaps this was a major one. It was a dark and stormy afternoon and shingles were flying off the neighbor's roof, resembling a spooked flock of blackbirds. The electric wires in the alley were dangling from the pole in the high wind, creating bright arcs as they neared the rain-soaked ground.

Everyone in the town had been urged to evacuate—the main fear being high water. Some went north to towns on higher ground, but most of our block went to Franklin Elementary School at the last minute. The only reason we were still at home was that Mary Jean, my sister, had diphtheria. We were all confined to sort of house arrest by the city nurse. "Quarantine" they called it on the sign tacked on the front porch.

I don't remember why that didn't include Sweetie, as my father was called. He was allowed to go to work. He had called the day before to tell us he wouldn't be home. The Gulf Refinery was going to put his unit on standby and they would have to ride out the storm there. His relief couldn't reach the plant due to high water. He was stuck there.

Mother wasn't afraid, or at least she didn't let on to us kids. When it grew dark, she lit a couple of candles and while she played the piano, she, Bill, and I sang along. This was her chance to play "Nearer My God to Thee" without our neighbor, Mrs. Felps, complaining that it reminded her of her mother's funeral. Mrs. Felps, whose hearing must have been very acute, never failed to ask Mother to stop playing that hymn.

Back then the dairy lobby in Washington got a law passed that you couldn't sell oleomargarine (oleo) without a ten-dollar permit. And, even with a permit, the oleo could not be yellow. We bought the oleo in one-pound blocks with a little envelope of orange powder. It was my job to mix the two together to make it look like butter. Since it was much cheaper than butter, and tasted about the same, oleo became a popular commodity during the Depression and thereafter.

We had few bank robberies. In those days they shot bank robbers instead of just taking their pictures. When caught in the act, they could not plead "not guilty" because of a rotten father or mother or child abuse. The judges and juries knew better than to fall for that.

One of the games we played was tin can shinny. It was like ice hockey without the ice. We used an empty evaporated milk can for a puck and made our sticks from oleander limbs. The shinny part happened if you got on the wrong side of the can; you could get hit on the shin with the opposing team's sticks.

It is true we didn't have all the things we wanted to eat, but we did not waste food. If someone offered ice cream or pie, we said, "Yes, please," not "What kind or what flavor."

DeQueen Elementary School was five blocks from the canal in Port Arthur. One day in the winter of 1929, it snowed. My classroom on the third floor had a southern exposure. Since snowing in Port Arthur was such a rare occasion, the students were so filled with expectations of snowball fights and building snowmen, we couldn't keep our minds on class. We took turns going to the pencil sharpener by the windows. It was on one of these "turns" I thought I saw a big sailing ship going up the canal toward Beaumont. No one believed me. When we looked at the *Port Arthur News* that evening, there it was, story and pictures of *Old Ironsides, the USS Constitution,* visiting the port of Beaumont.

Mr. Thibedeaux, a barber downtown, owned and staked out his cow each day in Gillum Circle. My first job paid twenty cents a week. I had to take that cow back to his house every day on my way home from school. One day the stake was harder than usual to pull up. I put down my books and my report card so I could use both hands. Well, you are not going to believe what that cow did. I turned around in time to see the last part of that pink, six-ply report card disappear into the cow's mouth. I have to admit I had mixed emotions about it. She ate my report card. I don't know how I explained that to my parents or my teacher.

One year a medicine show came to town. I must have been about seven or eight that year. The show was located on a corner vacant lot of Eleventh Street and Lake Charles Avenue, three blocks from our house. I didn't know what it was, but Sweetie, my father, was going, so I went too.

It didn't look like much, just an old man dressed in western garb on the back of a flat-bed truck, playing the banjo. The place was lighted and that, in addition to the noise, attracted a crowd of forty or fifty people.

After the man told a few jokes I didn't understand, he began to offer, free, his five dollar health book full of cure-alls, with each purchase of a bottle of this elixir for one dollar. I didn't think Sweetie was going to fall for that line, and he didn't at first. But, as the night wore on with more banjo playing and joke telling, Sweetie became more interested in the medicine. When some people got up on the truck and swore by the stuff, he gave in. By the time he bought the medicine, it was selling three bottles for a dollar minus the book.

I didn't know then that three pints of Three Sixes (heavily laced with quinine) mixed with that red medicine would last for years. This concoction became the replacement for castor oil at our house. That mixture was the kind of stuff that made you get up in the morning though sick as a dog, smile and go to school just to keep from having to take a dose of the foul smelling cure-all. Looking back, I remember I never suffered with malaria, and it did wonders for our school attendance record.

When Bobby Jacobs graduated from high school in 1941, he went to Nashville, Tennessee to start a career as an apprentice printer with the Nashville Banner. In late 1941 he joined the Navy, one step ahead of the draft board, and served three years, two months and ten days. When discharged he returned to Port Arthur, married his childhood sweetheart Helen Sudduth, and went to work in a job print shop running presses. Four years later he was approached by a life insurance company and offered a job in the life insurance business. After being transferred several times in the next fifteen years, he ended up in Phoenix, Arizona, and at age forty-two "got a real job". He worked in a power plant with great people and retired twenty years later. As one of the few who retired FROM Arizona, he returned to Texas as soon as he could. He is still married and happy living in Spring, Texas. His children are scattered. Pat lives and works in South Africa, Mike in Colorado, Erin in Connecticut and Pam is the only one left in Phoenix. All are married and doing well. He doesn't think he should be the one to ask when the Depression ended, but it did end for most folks after World War II.

DAVID K. HUGHES

Life in the Fast Lane
—Downtown Houston, 1935

I was eleven years old and my brother Harry, was ten when my father, an oil broker with offices in the Bankers Mortgage Building, moved us and our mother into a suite in the Milby Hotel in downtown Houston. My older brother and two sisters stayed on Cortland Street in the Heights with our grandparents.

At first, Harry and I really missed the Heights. It wasn't long before we really appreciated being downtown, six floors above all the action. The people, their different type clothes—the noise of the cars and trucks—in two weeks time we were walking all over the area.

Just across Travis Street on the west side was the Iris Theater. The entrance to the right of the Iris led to the Uptown Arcade, with marble tables and all kinds of games. The aisles swung west and then turned south and looking straight ahead we could see the Texan Theater.

Months later, after we learned our way around, we found a way of getting up to the roof of the Milby Hotel. What a view! We could see for miles! Northwest stood the Chronicle Building. West of that on Texas Avenue was the City Auditorium and the Auditorium Hotel. South of that on Travis was the Brazos Hotel. But most important of all was the Esperson Building, the second largest building in Houston in 1935.

From another side of the hotel we could see the Montgomery Ward building. Farther south on the west side of Main, stood the tallest building in Houston, the Gulf Building with its thirty-two floors.

The Borden Milk and Ice Cream Building was east on Texas Avenue. South of Borden was the Houston Press building. What really fascinated us was the view of the Union Station where trains from all over came and went. Sometimes we could hear the train bells clanging and the loud speaker roaring, "Leaving on Track Number One for Dallas, Forth Worth, Saint Louis, Chicago and all points east. The Silver Streak—all aboard—last call!" Unforgettable sounds.

Parked on tracks that paralleled the south side of the station on Texas Avenue was a large train-like car. The car, much larger than a streetcar, had its name painted in gold letters: Houston-Galveston Railroad. Everyone in Houston called it the "Interurban." Passengers could board it and in an hour and a half be at the seawall on the beautiful beach in Galveston.

From the Milby roof we could see the impressive front of the Rice Hotel. The streetcar stopped at the corner below us. A streetcar came by every fifteen minutes. Lines of people formed at this intersection of Travis and Texas Avenue.

The view from the rooftop excited us—it was as though we were seeing all the known world for the first time.

The rooftop provided such a vantage point for us, we decided not to waste it. Our lady friend at the Iris's popcorn counter gave us fifty cellophane bags like she used to fill with popcorn. We "borrowed" some rubber bands from our father's desk, and a soup ladle from our mother's kitchen. I carried the bucket of water and Harry carried our supplies to the roof.

It was August and very hot and humid. Luckily for the people below, nearly every building had awnings to shade the people walking or standing on the sidewalks. Our water bombs did not hit the people protected by the awnings, but certainly splashed on them. Harry took Travis Street and I took Texas Avenue. We fired our bombs at five minute intervals. We'd wait until the people quit searching the rooftop for the culprits. We did this for three days.

On the third day we discovered we could walk south on the roof of the hotel to the roof of the Montgomery Ward Building next door. There we could target the streetcar stop on Capitol and Travis also.

Later the broad smiles on our faces as we walked past some splashed-on streetcar riders quickly vanished when we were approached by a very tall and well-liked officer of Houston's "finest." His beat was the Rice Hotel at Texas and Main Street. Because of problems with his feet, Officer Reno was the only man on the Houston Police Force allowed to wear cowboy boots.

DAVID K. HUGHES

Officer Reno called out, "Hey, Harry, you and Dave come over here! I want to talk to you two." We looked at each other. "I'll do the talking," I said. "Okay?" "Okay." We walked up to Officer Reno.

Awed by this giant of a man my gift for gab left me. He did not speak for a few moments, merely stared down at us.

"Boys," he began, "it's come to my attention from numerous complaints that someone is dropping water bombs all over this town. You boys know anything about this?"

Standing rigid with an innocent look, I replied, "Oh, no sir, Mr. Reno. We sure don't."

"Well, let me put it this way, boys. If I hear any more complaints about water bombs, I'm throwing you two under the jail." He smiled, turned and walked away. There were no more complaints.

We heard we might be able to get jobs selling newspapers on the street. The HOUSTON POST was a morning edition and a late evening edition they called THE MIDNIGHT POST. THE CHRONICLE and THE PRESS were called "afternoon rags." When a big story broke between edition times the papers put out an EXTRA with big bold headlines. We would walk the streets yelling, "Extra! Extra! Read all about it!"

If the story was "extra" good, we would sell all our papers. Our largest selling EXTRA was the fateful day Wiley Post and Will Rogers' plane crashed in Alaska and both perished. This was the darkest day we had ever experienced. Every time I dried my eyes and would half-way straighten-up, a man or woman would buy a paper with tears on their faces, too. I would choke up and start crying again.

A few days later, a friend of our father asked him if we had faked the tears to sell more papers. "Hell, no," our father said. "The boys kept us up all night with their sobbing."

Kelley's Restaurant was a half block from our hotel. Kelley, the owner, wasn't an Irishman, but a Greek who had changed his name. There were dining areas in the restaurant, but the one we liked best was the stand-up oyster bar at the front of the building. We would sell enough newspapers until we made a dollar. Paul, our favorite oysterman, would open two dozen oysters (25 cents a dozen) for us. These were served with fresh horseradish, lemon, and all the crackers you could eat.

69

If you were a kid and lived in or around Houston in the 1930's, you knew or had heard of a man named Will Horwitz. He was a wonderful man who owned the Iris, Texan, and Uptown theaters. He was a Jewish American who had such a kind and giving heart, that our Dad, one of his close friends, called him O'Horwitz. "He's bound to have a little Irish in him, too," Dad said.

Once a year when school was out, Mr. Horwitz would advertise in all three newspapers a free pass to these theaters on a certain Saturday. Not only did the pass entitle the kid to the movie, but to all the peanuts, popcorn, and cold drinks a kid could handle.

The theaters would open at 7:00 a.m. instead of noon. No adults could attend. The theaters were opened until late afternoon so the kids could get home before dark. Lines of kids formed two abreast along Travis Avenue down to Texas Avenue.

Mr. Horwitz hired off-duty policemen to see that the kids had fun but didn't take up the entire sidewalk. Officer Reno, in his cowboy boots, seemed to enjoy his patrol. He said the kids were too excited to cause trouble. The kids loved him.

Up before dawn, we'd watch out the window to determine when it was time for us to join the line going into the Iris Theater. When we entered the theater, we saw small brown bags of roasted peanuts stacked to the ceiling. We were given a bag of peanuts, one of popcorn, and a cup of either Coke or root beer. The movie started at 8:00 a.m. It ended at 9:30 a.m. The ushers would empty the theater of this first group. The ones lined up outside would then be allowed in. This schedule went on until 5:00 p.m. when the theater would be closed.

The free movie with free peanuts, popcorn, drinks was not the only thing Mr. Horwitz did for the kids of Houston. Every Christmas he would hire a large hall and give toys, food and candy to underprivileged kids. After I was grown I learned that these two activities for children were the least of Mr. Horwitz's gifts to the people of Houston and Texas.

David K. Hughes was born in the Houston Heights, attended Reagan High School, joined the Navy at seventeen, almost a year before Pearl Harbor and was in a motor whaleboat four hundred yards from the USS Arizona when it blew up on December 7th. His ship USS Northampton (Heavy Cruiser) was in the battle "Midway", was with Doolittle on the Tokyo raid and later sunk at Guadalcanal. He had various jobs after the war, mainly in sales, Coca Cola, Dentler Potato Chips, beer business twenty-five years, and retired wholesale whiskey salesman for Penland Distributors, Houston. He's polishing his first fiction novel.

(5) l - r David K. Hughes age 11 & Harry B. Hughes age 10 - 1935

JEANA KENDRICK

Jim Kendrick Story

Waco During the Dark Days

"**I** really didn't know anybody who jumped out of a window when the stock market crashed in twenty-nine," said Jim Kendrick, recollecting the days of his youth spent in Waco, Texas. Even though he was only nine when the Depression hit, Jim recalls that stocks were going downhill fast, millions were being lost and it even got worse in the Thirties. Shares of General Motors and good wheat land in the Panhandle were sold for five dollars. You could probably buy any home in Waco for $25,000. The Cameron family mansion on Austin Avenue which cost $250,000 to build in the Twenties sold for $8,000 in 1941 and became the public library.

When Jim's dad lost his job as head coach at San Antonio's St. Mary's University in 1929, the family moved in with his Aunt Sue at Whitehall, a large white house in Waco. "Dad speculated in the oil business trying to make money and Mother taught elementary school," Jim said. "We had to cut the corners and not spend much money. Don't get me wrong now, we always had enough to eat, a roof over our head and a car to drive. Although movies were cheap, twenty-five cents, we didn't go. We listened to the radio, had parties at home and Mother played the piano for us."

In 1934 Jim's Grandmother Evans died and they inherited his mother's large family home on Colcord Avenue. Jim, his parents and three younger brothers lived downstairs, and the upstairs was divided into apartments they rented. Eventually, they took in roomers downstairs and finally boarders, which meant hiring a cook and serving three hot meals a day. Meanwhile, Jim's dad traveled buying and selling oil leases across Texas, while his mother continued to teach.

According to Jim the whole family worked and scraped and saved to buy a green deluxe Ford sedan in 1935 for $550. "We

73

(6) Jimmy Kendrick age 20

thought it was the greatest," he said. "It had two tail lights, two horns and chrome trim. Back then hamburgers sold for ten cents and bottled coke for a nickel. Common labor was twenty-five cents an hour."

People experienced varying degrees of hardship and those less fortunate often smiled at the problems besetting the rich. In Waco the Davis' were known for their lovely mansion and high style of living. So when Mr. Davis went from bank to bank, trying to borrow money for living expenses with his wife's jewels as collateral, everyone knew things were plenty rough. Jim also remembers his Aunt Clara's in-laws, near millionaires who lost much of their wealth in the real estate crisis of 1929, exclaiming, "And to think, Clara, we have to wear five dollar shoes." Similarly, Dr. John Brinkley, infamous for implantation of goat glands to rejuvenate his patients, sparked headlines which read "Hard Times - the Brinkley Family Down to Last Four Cadillacs."

Happily for the Kendricks, their fortune changed in 1937 when they struck it rich from some productive oil leases his dad had purchased. "When we made the money Mother quit teaching. She redid the house and that ended the boarders and roomers, but she continued to rent the upstairs apartments because we didn't need all that space," said Jim. "The lower floor was big enough for us. Mother already owned a farm and Dad expanded it from sixty acres to two-hundred-twenty. And we bought another new car."

Later that year, the family accompanied Jim's dad East on a business trip where seventeen-year-old Jim contracted polio. By then there was plenty of money for doctors, but they soon learned that the doctors knew little about the treatment of polio. For four months Jim remained semi-paralyzed with his future health a grave question mark. Despite his sickness his mother insisted that Jim continue with his school work. She was determined Jim would graduate with his class.

Gradually, Jim recovered and graduated with his high school class in 1939, the year Hitler invaded Poland. To celebrate graduation, his mother allowed Jim to host an all night party for his class. The neighbors a block away couldn't sleep for the noise. But no one thought to complain; they sat up through the night reading.

Two years later Jim's father invested in oil leases that were not productive and the money started running out. Once again his mother taught school and times were rough. Then in 1941, the same year as Pearl Harbor, Jim's dad died. They sold one of the cars and all four boys got jobs. Jim was nineteen and in his sophomore year at Baylor University. "After my father died the cook and the hired help were let go. I raised pigs, milked cows and repaired fences on Aunt Sue's farm," Jim said. "Mother rented out our farm for two dollars an acre. It paid the mortgage payment with a little left over. Mother would say, 'If I can just get through January, I can get through anything,' because all the bills and taxes were due then."

Jim graduated early in April 1943 with a business degree from Baylor University. Immediately, he joined the Air Force. After a year of training he departed with blackout orders in effect on an unescorted former luxury liner with seven thousand other Americans for New Guinea and the Philippines. There he served as a cryptographer, decoding secret messages. When the men came down with malaria they were given drugs to suppress it until the war ended. On New Year's Eve 1946 Jim arrived home via the Bonhomme Richard aircraft carrier. After a bout with malaria he returned to Baylor for a degree in law. Following graduation he married Baylor homecoming queen Elaine Bush and accepted a job as landman with Amoco Production Company.

"Looking back on the days of the Depression, I realize that many conservative values were established. My Uncle John T, a conservative banker, influenced me greatly. One of my most vivid impressions was seeing four of my uncles, willing to work, but unable to find full-time, gainful employment. I was impressed to work hard and to save money in order to have capital. The old adage, a full day's pay for a full day's work, became a guide by which I lived," Jim said.

Despite the hardships of war and the Depression, growing up in Waco in the Thirties and Forties, provided an optimum environment, according to Jim. "Society was stable. Families stayed together and were usually extended since uncles, aunts and cousins lived nearby. Divorce was rare and crime was low; moral value and church attendance was high. The standard of living was low as compared to the Eighties," Jim said, "but it was adequate. There was little pollution and no drugs, but a lot of outdoor activities prevailed. America was at peace and the church, school and family were in control. With these factors, there was the desire to excel, to be productive, by getting an education or learning a trade and then going to work. This all provided a powerful motivation to reach one's potential, and most did."

After the Depression, Jim Kendrick received his BBA and JD at Baylor. Served in the military: SWPA as cryptographer and JAG, Air Force. He has been happily married forty-nine years with four children, six grandchildren and one great grandchild. He was the Division Landman for a major oil firm, and is still an active independent. He has held numerous titles on boards and committees. His eldest Jeff married Jeana Kendrick, Communications Director and Managing Editor for *Door of Hope International.*

MARGARET MONTGOMERY

Depression: What Depression?

The Great Depression didn't greatly depress me. How could it? Wasn't I a brand new bride married to the man I loved who was feathering our nest in Palestine ("Two-gun Kelly's" little rent house) with $115.00 a month's worth of feathers?

Our friends were well-off too and almost every Saturday night we met in somebody's home, played high stakes (dime limit) poker and ate spaghetti fixed more ways that Skinner or McCormick's dreamed possible. None of us in the regular group soon forgot the night that one of our members brought in a city slicker from Chicago who it was reported made two hundred dollars a month selling Betty Bet Dresses For The Discerning Woman, top price $9.95, who cleaned us of almost five dollars, bringing on a local hiatus until pay day.

The small town where we lived was "dry" but our husbands were creative. From a newspaper ad they ordered a recipe from some place in California for mixing their "secret ingredients" with grapes, which grew abundantly in our area, to produce "an exotic wine."

Following their urging, our husbands stored the filled half-gallon jars of "makin's" in Hank and Bernice's rarely used storeroom to age. When the bottles blew up plastering the ceiling and sides of the storeroom with exotic secret ingredients and fermented grapes, both Bernice and their dog Boris had a fit, although Bernice didn't run in circles and howl.

I knew, of course, that somewhere people ate Hoover chicken (rabbit, possum), that men stuffed newspapers in their ragged clothes for warmth, and that my mother instructed her cook to keep well seasoned black-eyed peas and cornbread on hand to feed the many hungry "hobos" who came to our back door, but I personally was never hungry or cold.

I do remember taking one of Rob's old suits (old? all of his suits were old) to Mr. Wacha, a genial, smiling tailor who was apparently born with a tape line around his neck, to cut down into a suit for me. Many of my friends did the same with their husband's old suits. After strategic openings and closings with his magic scissors, the suits reappeared with the shiny pants turned inside out into a skirt and with the still a bit too broad in the shoulders jacket revealing a jabot instead of a shirt and tie. We "brides" told each other that we were irresistible but we lied. The sad truth was that we looked like wedge-shaped members of some weird cult.

Time passed and when Rob's salary was increased to $175.00 a month, we rented a better house and ordered our first child, Robert Montgomery, Jr., to share the wealth.

Since the Great Depression, Margaret Montgomery has rafted white water on the Arkansas River, lived in six states, raised three teenagers, Bob, Dan and Jane, lived through one earthquake, one tornado, the grand opening of a supermarket. She has written dozens of columns for newspapers and magazines, won one international essay contest (Rotarian Magazine) one state contest (Associated Country Women of the World), and has never taken a pill for "depression." Quite a party she says!

HERBERT PETERS

Meanwhile, Back at the Ranch

Some pre-Depression years before I was born (I showed up near the end of December, 1929—great timing!), my mom and dad had built a little house about half a block away from her mother's house in Sabinal, Texas. At some point, that dwelling burned down. Henceforth, when living back in Sabinal or spending summers there, the family would live at Nana's, but often the whole family or just the kids would undertake excursions to the "Ranch", belonging to my other grandmother, but more about that later.

One of the most pervasive misconceptions about the Depression was that most people were on the verge of starvation. I think it's because the old newsreels and other movies often shown about that period were concentrated on the "hungry" and "breadlines" found in the larger cities. Most of America was rural; they lived either in a small town or on a farm or a parcel of land on which a garden could be planted that provided most of what they needed. The fare was limited to what would grow where they lived, but a small food budget would usually suffice to augment the local product. Therefore, only a small percentage of the population was in real need: the aforesaid urban centers and the victims of the "Dust Bowl" disaster.

The kids, particularly the younger ones, didn't know the difference. What you ate was what you were accustomed to seeing on the table, so they didn't consider themselves "deprived." If supper was corn meal mush a couple of times a week, you didn't question. Also, you didn't express dislike for certain foods you'd see a lot. Otherwise, you would be "excused" from further "torture" and believe me, when the same food showed up again, you generally ate it with gusto.

One example I recall was one evening when my sister inquired what we were going to have for supper. "Beans and cornbread," she was told. The "beans" of course meant pintos. When Sister said she didn't like that, Mama said, "All right; just for you we'll have Gobble-Goodie." This turned out to be buttered cornbread soaked in a soupy bowl of beans. Sister loved it, and despite its silly name, it became one of our family's standard meals; it's still one of *my* favorites!

Many times, out of necessity, dishes that were normally considered breakfast items were served for supper, such as oatmeal, or one of the following.

Corn meal mush was basically just meal, boiled with butter added. It was served in a big cup, with a spoon and some cold milk. It was one of those foods that seem to hold their heat forever, like baked apples. Anyway, you'd take a small amount of mush on the spoon, dip it in the cold milk, and wait even a bit longer before trying it. Many were the times I burned my tongue on mush because little kids don't seem to understand waiting until something cools.

Another cereal-based, and therefore cheap, meal was porridge for breakfast. This was a favorite because of the tie-in with Goldilocks and her ursine hosts. It was just graham flour, boiled until cooked. The closest thing today is Malt-O-Meal. We used to fix it frequently when my own kids were growing up, but now graham flour is impossible to find. It must still exist, as graham crackers are made from it, but I've tried many forms of ground whole wheat and none have the semi-sweet flavor of the original.

My wife was a Houston native, and to her family, rice was something salty you doused with a "meat and gravy" dish, a function our tribe reserved for potatoes. In near-west Texas, however, rice was a cereal, served for breakfast with butter, sugar, and cream.

But old food preferences die hard, and I would still rather have it that way, although since discovering Louisiana's "rice and red beans," I eat a lot of it that way, too.

Whether in town or at the Ranch, one day a week was devoted to making bread. "Lightbread" with a meal seemed to be more important in those days than now. There was nothing like the aroma of bread baking. As soon as the first loaf came out, it was turned out to be tested.

My cousins and I thought the tastiest thing in the world was yellow mustard spread on a slice still hot from the oven. We were often admonished not to do that, as bread was supposed to be cooled before consumption. I guess now it had something to do with allowing the carbon dioxide formed by the yeast to evaporate before the loaf was eaten. However, it must not have been too important, as we always seemed to get away with swiping a hot slice and eating it as described, and we survived.

At the Ranch, which supported a few Jersey cows, there was more emphasis on milk products. Since there was always some that had soured, a cheesecloth sack of clabber was usually hanging in some tree to drip and dry enough to be made into cottage cheese, known locally as "cream cheese." A dish of this as well as a plate of sliced tomatoes was *always* on the table along with the condiments.

One day when I was in my early teens, an older cousin and I were left alone at the Ranch while the remainder of the household went into town for staples and ice. We discovered to our delight that there was a lot of milk and cream in the ice box, which we decided shouldn't be allowed to go bad. So we dug out the old orange, hand-cranked freezer and made it full of ice cream. As I recall, it held about six gallons. For variety, we colored it blue and called it "Blue Sky" ice cream. We threw in a quantity of little marshmallows as "clouds." We ate on our creation all day until the rest of the family returned. They finished it up as dessert after supper, although by that time we weren't too interested in additional food!

There was always heavy cream, too, which, when *it* soured, was churned into butter. The buttermilk left from this procedure was *thin* and delicious. I have no idea why commercial buttermilk is made thick, and has little of the delightful flavor of what was left in a churn.

Foods that grew easily thereabouts were the usual staples. One of my favorites was okra, boiled with onions, so it was all nice and slimy. Nobody out there ever heard of frying it or adulterating it with tomatoes.

The same was true with onions, which hung on a wire rack so they wouldn't spoil, squash (the roundish white kind), and whatever manner of green beans and greens that were in season at the time.

Throughout my boyhood, I recall that at every house to which we moved, which was many in several cities, Daddy would always plant himself a little garden. These varied in size and crop content, but the constants were Kentucky Wonder green beans and Swiss Chard. We ate lots of that.

In order to save perishable vegetables or fruit, a practice known as "canning" was used, which had nothing whatsoever to do with cans. The containers were large Mason jars, whose lids were in two parts: the actual top which had a ring of gray rubbery stuff around the edge that would ultimately form a tight seal with the edge of the jar, and a threaded ring by which the true lid was held on, at first rather loosely.

The "canning" process was conducted on the enormous wood-burning cooking stove, in a pressure cooker at least a foot and a half in diameter and over two feet high. The filled jars would be placed in the cooker until it came to a boil; then the top was secured. There were gauges on the top of the cooker which had to be watched closely to avoid the whole thing blowing up.

When the proper temperature and pressure had been reached for however long was required, the cooker was removed from the fire and allowed to cool a little while, just until the pressure dropped to permit opening it. The still almost boiling hot jars would be removed, and the rings screwed down, so the tops were held tightly in place as soon as possible. Further cooling within the jars would produce a slight vacuum, which helped keep the lids from developing air leaks, which would allow spoilage of the contents.

Also at the Ranch, periodic family "get togethers" would bring up to fifty or so relatives. It was a big, rambly house on the "high-bank" side of the river that had grown by years of accretion, so everybody seemed to be able to find a place to sleep.

For big family Bar-B-Qs like this, a big pit would be dug and filled with mesquite logs the night before, so by next morning it was full of fragrant coals. One of the wild Mexican goats whose presence was tolerated for this purpose, would be slaughtered and barbecued over those coals. This is a consummate delicacy, much better than the "cabrito" served in Mexican restaurants.

A great deal has been said about the hobos of that period who were indigent and homeless, but looking for jobs with which to support themselves, or, more often, families. Many had nothing but their dignity, a quality seemingly absent from most of today's homeless and/or welfare recipients. We didn't see

84

much of them, as they tended to congregate in industrial centers where the chances of finding permanent employment were greater. But occasionally, some man (*never* a woman) would appear at the doorstep seeking work for food. My grandmothers or whoever was at home would always find, and if necessary, manufacture some task so that got the guy fed, but didn't destroy his pride.

When the government Civilian Conservation Corps was established, many good and lasting public works were the result. Garner State Park in the north end of the county is such an example of well earned support by residents at CCC camps.

There seemed to be an unusual affinity for aviation in our little town. One day, an aeroplane developed some problem while flying in the vicinity and landed *right on Center Street!*— the only relatively flat expanse of sufficient length in the area. People swarmed out like bees from a disturbed hive to get a better look at this strange sight, and "Kodaks" clicked like katydids on a summer night. My sister's old picture album contains several photographs of the plane on the street.

I have no idea whether anybody other than me witnessed another incident. One day, I was lying on the decorative concrete end of the front steps at Nana's house, when I heard a curious droning sound. I looked up, and there was the Graf Zeppelin majestically flying over me. As I recall, there was a cross-country trip by this magnificent flying machine, and this would have been the leg of the journey from Brooks Field in San Antonio to somewhere in the west. Brooks Field was a base for lighter-than-air craft and had voluminous hangars in which they could be stored, whether rigid ships or blimps.

The airship was flying so low that I could see faces peering out of the gondola's windows. The edge of the Edwards Plateau, the southern border of the Hill Country in which all the local rivers originated, was about twenty miles north of us, so I suppose that's why they chose to fly over our relatively flat plain. It certainly wasn't the scenery, which was directly lacking. I know, as I have flown over the same path in a helicopter at a similarly low altitude, and it's pretty featureless. It isn't until you get to the mountains in far West Texas that any really interesting landscape is found, like the cluster of small volcanic craters just west of El Paso. You can only see these on an approach to the airport from the west. When last I heard, the owner continued to bar entrance to his property, even strewing the road with tacks to discourage visitors.

Both Grandpas were pretty well fixed, having made their money in ranching and related enterprises. Unfortunately, each owned a bank, and felt the duty to keep them solvent during the Depression. Grandpa Wish had also owned substantial land in the county, some of which he managed for the heirs of his mother-in-law's estate. This is where the Ranch came from; it was the legacy of his wife, Birdie Wish (Nana). He also administered his "daughter," Lillian's property, acquired from her mother, Belle, which was just across the river and down a ways from Nana's. Lillian lived at the Ranch after she and her husband lost a large part of their land which had been pledged behind some unfortunate investment.

That's where we went as kids in the summertime. How well do I remember sitting up late into the night, fiddling with their crystal radio. And how amazing it was to be able to move the little whisker to the right place and pick up music from Chicago! It was only years later that we began actively using Nana's part of the land, primarily because there was no house on it until one was built by hunting lessors.

My other grandpa also had a dry goods store which supported the family, at least for awhile. When times got really bad, it became apparent that the store would support only one family, so it was left with the elder brother, and the younger ones sought a living elsewhere. One went with the bank, and my daddy became an employee of the then fledgling Department of Alcohol and Firearms. I remember how impressed I was by his big old .45 automatic. He must have had to buy it himself, as it was covered with nicks and scratches. It wasn't too bad a deal, I guess, because it still functions well for my son today.

Later, but I don't know when, he was transferred to a newly established agency, the Internal Revenue Service, for whom he worked until his retirement. Over the years, various assignments required moving from city to city a lot, and our finances necessitated frequent moves within a given town.

When I was only about three, we moved to San Antonio for something less than two years. Then he was transferred to Corpus Christi, where we lived in eight places in just a couple of years.

I shall never forget our arrival in Corpus. It was at night, and it seemed to take forever to cross the causeway in our 1934 green Ford. We had temporary lodgings in an apartment only a couple of blocks from Ocean Drive, beyond which was the beach. I was only four at the time, but eager to see the water, so the next morning, I struck out in that direction. Unfortunately for my adventure, Mama noticed my absence almost immediately and called Daddy. Imagine my chagrin when I looked toward downtown just as I went over the high bank edge and saw the Ford bearing down upon me at a high rate of speed. I hurried down the path to the surf and had just arrived when a relieved but irate father came hustling down the path after me!

I got my "revenge," however. One evening a few days later, we were on one of the little piers, the long L and T heads not having been built yet, when the pilot of a small craft told Daddy he was going out to the gasoline station a little distance out in the Gulf for fuel, and would I like to ride along. Daddy said, "Okay," so off I went, riding with my legs dangling over the side of the boat. Mother, who hadn't heard the negotiations, was horrified. There was her baby boy heading out to sea with someone completely unknown. I was not around to hear the ensuing conversation, but I gather it was a dilly. Meanwhile, I was having a ball, singing a little song and feeling the boat rock as it took on fuel. We got back in good shape about half an hour later. I was most pleased with the excursion. Mother was not.

When I was in junior high and a couple of years of high school, we lived in Waco, in only three places, a record low for that length of time. One house had an alley running along the side of it which also contained the bedrooms. Only about four feet separated the house from the fence from the alley.

One night, a burglar picked our house as a target; I can't imagine why, as we lived in a relatively low income area, and there was nothing of large value in evidence. Unfortunately for him, the window he picked to enter was in Sister's room, and the bed ran right across the window for maximum breeze. Apparently in the dim light, he couldn't see it, either.

When he was about half way through the screen, she awoke and emitted a screech that was, I'm sure, audible for blocks. I don't know who was the more scared. All I *do* know is that he was back through the window screen in roughly two seconds, and made a run down the alley that would surely have qualified him for the Olympics. I feel certain that thereafter, he adopted another profession.

This was also the house where I was sprawled on the living room floor reading the Sunday funnies when the news came over the radio about the bombing of Pearl Harbor. We immediately had a lengthy family discussion on the ramifications of the attack and its ultimate effect on the country. I remember Mama shaking her head and saying, "Well, there goes the last of the Depression, but at what a price."

Herbert N. Peters was born on December 29, 1929 in San Antonio, Texas. He moved all around Texas from Sabinal to Corpus Christi to Waco following his father's assignments with the Bureau of Alcohol and Firearms. He graduated from Brackenridge High School in San Antonio, did a two-year stint in the Navy, attended Rice Institute and received a BA in Pre-Med in 1952. He married Catherine Clark in 1952 and moved to San Antonio. There, he worked seventeen years at the Alamo National Bank, was an advertising manager for several companies then did free lance creative services. He had four children. He always followed the arts, his great love being music, composing and performing with his wife and children. He wrote individual wedding marches for his children. He was also a photographer, painter, sculptor (his work is in many homes and public areas in San Antonio). He moved to Spring, Texas in 1989 and died on September 17, 1995. His family misses him dearly!

PAT POLAND

Making Do

I remember from childhood days in Grapeland...food being scarce and recycling everything. Nothing was thrown away. We raced empty spools of thread on the uneven back porch. Tin cans and jar lids made wonderful pretend dishes. If a shirt or pants no longer fit or couldn't be passed down to another family member, then we cut it apart as quilt pieces. The buttons were cut off and zippers were saved.

No boxed cakes or meals were to be had. Everything was made from recipes. And if you really were hungry, leftovers were eaten with thanks. I remember when food was really scarce...bread and catsup had to suffice. Luckily, I came from a family of hunters. So many times meat was the kill or catch of the day. I've eaten many a share of fried squirrel, baked duck and dressing, and fried venison. Summertime brought a storehouse of catfish and bass. We never killed what we couldn't eat.

We never bought jelly. There were plenty of muscadine grapes and blackberries for jelly, jam, juice and cobblers. The garden was bountiful. It yielded Irish potatoes, greens, onions, melons, corn, tomatoes, squash, okra, cantaloupes, peas, beans and beets. All of which were eaten, canned, frozen or bartered.

Grandma and Grandpa Parker had cows for milk, pigs for bacon, and chickens for eggs. If the chickens didn't lay, they got recycled and became chicken dinner. The pig eventually was slaughtered for the meat. The fresh bacon, sausage and pork chops were often referred to as "good ol' Porky."

My grandparents' farm was self-sufficient. Rarely did we ever trek to town. Store-bought milk was unheard of until the cow died of old age. We even churned our butter.

There wasn't any air-conditioning. The cracks in the clapboards and floorboards, along with the opened windows and doors, allowed enough air in to cool us. We'd turn on the box fan only in the dead of summer to help the breeze along. In the winter we had the heat from the stove and the gas heaters. Those same cracks in the walls and floors were chinked with newspapers to keep out the cold north winds.

I can only remember buying flour, sugar, gum, candy, coffee and tea from Darsey's. And of course, an occasional package of toilet paper for those visitors who refused to recycle the Houston Post the "farm way." There were times I remembered wishing that Grandpa Parker would recycle the old red rooster who chased me to the outhouse and back. Seems he annexed the grounds that building sat on as part of the hen house property. I made sure that the water I washed my hands with in the mornings gave him a cold bath for all his territorial behavior toward me.

At the end of garden season, we even saved some of the seeds, dried onions and let some potatoes turn to seed. No need to go to the feed store again for garden seed. Potato peelings fed the chickens in-between corn-feedings.

There were no dryers except the sun for the clothes, even in the winter. Sometimes we'd bring in clothes frozen stiff on the clothes-lines from a blue norther that blew in. We'd stand them, like frozen soldiers, in front of the gas heaters to dry.

Yes, I remember parts of the Depression, even though I'm a baby boomer, born after World War II. Times weren't the greatest, but we never needed food stamps or Medicaid.

Pat Poland is now a contracted freelance correspondant for The Houston Chronicle This Week/Montgomery County. She formerly worked as editorial staff writer for the Bulletin until August 1997.

MYRL MILLER

The Dust Bowl

Shortly before the stock market Crash, Daddy and his brother Claude quit their jobs as bookkeepers (they weren't called accountants back then) at Cameron Lumber Company in Clarendon, Texas and Altus, Oklahoma respectively, borrowed money, took their new brides, and opened a Piggly Wiggly grocery store in Quitaque, Texas. On a recent television program, I heard a nearby Turkey, Texas citizen named Otho Stubbs say that the area was booming in the late Twenties. So maybe that's why they chose to move to a place neither of them had ever lived before.

The grocery business would seem to be a safe place to ride out hard times, even if they lasted several years, since everyone has to eat. But groceries were bought on credit, and when the banks closed in 1933—some permanently, even the wealthiest man in the county couldn't pay his bill. Then the drought hit and no crops meant no cash. Daddy recalled going out with some other townsmen to a widow's house, where they found several hungry children and nothing in the house to eat but salt and pepper. He went back to the store and gathered up apples, beans and a few staples to tide her over until something more permanent could be done for her. But he couldn't keep feeding the whole town for long.

Before the Depression my Grandfather Miller had a small farm in north-central Texas, which he leased out, and a large farm near Quanah where they lived during the summer— Grandmother and the younger children lived in town during the school year. The farm had a tennis court, croquet green, orchard, and the usual livestock and farming equipment. They also had several cars— he had lost everything and had to move his family for one year to a small rented farm with an ugly unpainted house. They started all over with a small dairy, bartering eggs, milk and

91

butter at the grocery store in town for flour and other staples. It was a bad time for raising crops, and there were no farm subsidies, no crop insurance. My grandparents and the three offspring still at home scratched out a living and managed to have enough extra to take in various of the married offspring who one by one had to retreat to the nest when their own jobs dried up. When Granddaddy died thirty years later, he was a comfortably prosperous man again, having worked very hard without complaint to regain at least some of what they had lost.

My other grandfather had at least eight farms spread out in at least five counties that I know of, and a large house in Clarendon, where they lived. He was able to maintain a comfortable standard of living despite the hard times. He died in 1936, and my grandmother took over the management of all that far-flung property—a big job for someone who didn't know how to drive. She did try to learn, but the day she lost control and ended up in somebody's front yard, she gave up for good. So her children often returned home on weekends to take her around the countryside to check on the farms.

Finally, the worsening drought, coupled with the lingering Depression and the death of his brother Claude, did Daddy in. My Grandfather Benson had loaned him some money to keep going, but there was no way he could continue. By that time, he and Mother had a child and a mountain of debt. He took my mother and me to Quanah, to stay with his parents, while he went to look for a job. Ironically, while all of Oklahoma was emptying out, heading west in search of jobs, he found one in Frederick, Oklahoma, as bookkeeper for his old employer, Cameron Lumber Company. The job paid eighty dollars a month.

In the beginning we took only my baby bed and lived for a few weeks in a bedroom of a Mrs. Huffine's house, where we had boarding privileges and the use of her living room. Soon they found a little old house near downtown that Mother later described as a terrible dump. It was so near a hotel that its neon sign flashed on and off all night, keeping them awake.

Within a month or so they found a better house on an elm-lined street: 1011 North 12th Street, a stucco house that still looks about the same as it did then. The rent was twenty-five dollars a month, but because it was roomy and Daddy was a clever man, he was able to build a free-standing kitchen cabinet for one of the two glassed-in sleeping porches and convert it into a sunny kitchen and sitting room. We rented out the side of the house where the two bedrooms were, used the dining room for our bedroom—my baby bed sat in one corner and the dining room suite was relegated to the other glassed-in porch—and we may have all shared one bathroom. We rented out the "apartment" for twenty-five dollars a month and so had our house free.

In addition, there was a servants' quarters facing onto the alley—as there was with most of the houses in town, no matter how humble—which we let out to couples in exchange for maid's work and occasional yard work. The quarters were separated from our back yard by a chicken-wire fence.

We had a very large side yard to the west, on which Daddy tried to grow vegetables, but the dust storms were so strong that everything would be covered completely in sand after a big blow. One year my parents decided to raise chickens instead, to augment our grocery budget, but this turned out to be a disaster. The chickens got some sort of disease that caused them to peck each other to death.

The black dust boiled up from the northwest periodically, usually in the spring. It covered up fence posts and even whole cars. It turned the day into night, obliterating sun and street lights. It sifted under window sills, even though people put wet towels across the sills to seal them: in a few hours the towels would be coated red or black, and the inside air would be hazy.

It could be dangerous to be caught outside in a sandstorm. The dirt killed livestock and people indiscriminately. And the whine of the wind during a sandstorm sounded like the howls of disembodied coyotes. The wind never completely died away during certain seasons. Even in its less blustery stage, it kept up a persistent low moan. I have read that pioneer women, left home alone on the prairie for weeks while the menfolk drove the cattle to market, often went insane, hearing nothing but that mournful wail, day and night with no let-up.

Because Frederick lies in "tornado alley," in the back yard was a storm cellar with a concrete top that made a great stage after I started tap lessons. (Every mother had aspirations to turn out another Shirley Temple, and at great financial sacrifice, gave their tykes tap lessons almost as soon as they could walk.)

Mother didn't like storm cellars, which she said were crawling with Daddy Longlegs, but she told our maid Savannah that she and her husband were welcome to use it anytime.

One night a terrible storm boiled up with green clouds and stinging sand, and Daddy grabbed me up and told Mama to head for the cellar. They ran out into the wind and Daddy managed to get the door up with me clinging to the top of his head from my perch on his shoulders. As they started down the dark cellar stairs, all I could see below were white eyeballs all around the room. The small space was packed to overflowing: it was the night of a big Joe Louis fight, and Savannah and her husband had invited all their friends over to our cellar to listen to the fight on a radio which had been plugged into the one overhead light socket. Because of some code of the times having to do with segregation, my parents backed out of the cellar and took their chances with the storm. In later years, Mother said of that dangerous night, "If it'd just been our own people, I might've gone on down."

I can't imagine whose radio they had; radios were very scarce. We didn't have one ourselves for a very long time, for we weren't likely to have anything we couldn't pay cash for. The first one I ever heard was at my Aunt Vivian's house in Hereford. I thought there were tiny people inside, talking into a big microphone like I had seen in the movies. My grandparents had a radio, but they used it sparingly, as if it might wear out if it were turned on. There was some validity in this, for radios were full of tubes that burned out like light bulbs.

Finally we got a Zenith—it may have been second-hand, but it was a very nice walnut curved Art-Deco radio. It is still a handsome radio to this day. I have it in my home, and it still works, old original vacuum tubes and all. After we got it, my parents spent their evenings sitting around it, listening to the whole night's line-up. Daddy knew the schedule by heart and at suppertime announced what was on both the red and blue networks of NBC, as well as what was on CBS and the Mutual Network.

As soon as I learned to read—which was very early, Mama took me down to the store and bought textbooks, which anyone could buy, for the State of Oklahoma did not furnish school books. They were beautiful hardback books, wonderful books, which I have to this day. The most special was an art book, with great colored pictures. I must have read that book easily a hundred times over the years. The price is marked inside: it cost forty-five cents.

One of the pictures was of autumn leaves. I had never seen such beautiful leaves, for Chinese elm leaves just turn brown and drop off without ceremony. But after I read the book, I discovered a few sycamore trees across the street, whose leaves, if not beautifully red, were at least an interesting shape and somewhat more colorful than elm leaves. I scuffed through them and figured that was as near as I would ever get to beautiful leaves.

There was also a story about colorful birds, and a picture of bluejays and cardinals. I decided the colors must be exaggerated. The only birds hardy enough to survive in the Dust Bowl were sparrows. Just as fantastic to me was a picture of a squirrel with an acorn. Not only did I never expect to see a squirrel, I didn't think I would ever see an acorn or an oak tree, or colorful leaves or colorful birds. They were all like the castles and princesses in my story books; they had existed in another time and another place.

Daddy was very musical and loved to dance. He had always wanted to learn to tap, and one way he justified the expense of my lessons was that I was to come home after each lesson and teach him my new steps. He had aspirations of being another Fred Astaire.

But his dancing lessons were cut short: he became very ill. I would come home from lessons and want to show him my steps, and he would tell me in a weak voice from his bed in our dining room that he would have to catch up later. As there were no antibiotics, Daddy grew more gravely ill and almost died. It seems that he was in the hospital for a while, but he was sent home, no better. Probably he ran out of money for hospital care.

One day Mr. Paul Gaither, the district manager of Daddy's company, came to our house. I waited outside the French doors to the bed/dining room and listened. Mr. Gaither stood at the foot of the bed and said, "Jimmy, do you think you'll get well enough to become the new manager of the Clarendon yard?"

Mama brightened and even Daddy's voice seemed a little stronger. He said, "I'll get well enough, all right."

And from that day onward, he began to improve. It was quite a promotion, because it came with a new company car every year or so. Besides, Clarendon was Mama's hometown. It was where Daddy was working when she and Daddy met, and they had a large circle of friends. It was the turn in our fortunes that he and Mama had waited for.

Later, he would move on to other, more promising things and eventually become his own boss. But at the time, the job as manager of the Cameron Lumber Company seemed the most wonderful thing that could possibly happen for us all.

I recall one day after we had moved when I assessed my situation and decided that I was the luckiest person on earth. First, I was born white, which even at my age I realized made all the difference in my fortunes. Second, I was born female: I wouldn't have to go into the army when I grew up, and I wouldn't have to leave home and go to work. I would be cherished by somebody all my life. Third, I lived in the very best town, in the very best state, in the best country on earth. Fourth, I lived in mythic times; I was experiencing it *all*. Not only had I met my great-grandfather who had fought in the Civil War, I had uncles who had been in World War I. I was experiencing the Dust Bowl and the Depression first-hand. When Japan attacked Pearl Harbor, I excitedly ran to record it in my diary, adding, "I have never been in a war before." This I equated in importance with the recent magical arrival of a baby sister.

We had movies, a radio, a library, Vacation Bible School, summer vacations: a Fourth of July parade and a picnic with homemade peach ice cream. We had the wonders of Christmas, of which we weren't reminded until after Thanksgiving. We spent holiday evenings caroling to the neighbors—the same ones we'd earlier hit for "Trick or Treat." Sunday visits with relatives and summer trips to see cousins reminded us that we were part of a giant web of relationships, a tribe, a clan—a safety net of sorts which was central to our feeling of security in those uncertain times.

When I was older, I read that I had lived in the most desolate spot in the country during its most wretched economic period. According to history books, I should have been miserable. But we were much more fortunate than the wealthiest children today, who are separated by half a continent from relatives they

(7) l-r Ina, Jimmy, Myrl Miller

may never know, and abjured from leaving the safety of their own turf because of a variety of perils. Besides, everyone in our town was in the same boat then, so nobody felt unjustly deprived.

Life in the Dust Bowl taught me a thing or two about appreciating beauty. Every single morning I marvel at the colorful birds, the great oaks and pines, the squirrels, all things I never thought I would ever see. The thrill of seeing them now is something I don't get over—and don't ever want to get over. I don't need world travel to experience wondrous things; there are enough to awe me on my own block.

The Depression years and the lean war years that followed also taught me lessons, learned from observing my parents, about frugality, caution, patience, the temporality of worldly goods, the fickleness of "prosperity" as a goal, the closeness and preciousness and dependability of family—I cherished that new addition to ours as no baby sister has ever been cherished. Those years made me more discerning about what's important enough to spend my money or my time on. They made me ambitious, but they were a reminder that ambition doesn't always yield permanent results, so they made me tolerant of failure—in myself and others. And they made me cognizant of the luck of the draw.

My draw was pretty great. I wouldn't trade with anyone.

After college Myrl Miller married and became a teacher. She had four children, three of whom married and produced grandchildren. About the only complaints she had about her children had to do with their being wasteful and careless about money. The family enjoyed a very comfortable living, but she was quite miserly with the children. She is not sure she's sorry. They learned to work for what they wanted and turned out very well. They learned to share and are close to each other and to their parents. Myrl wonders what more could any mother want?

ZENAIDE MC DANIEL

The First Depression

The happiest day of my life was October 13, 1928 in Houston, Texas. That was the day I married Mac. I was twenty and very much in love with this wonderful man.

Mac was employed at the Great Southern Life Insurance Company. His salary was $250.00 a month in 1928. He said, "Naide, now we can get married. I feel that two-hundred-fifty dollars a month is enough for us to marry and live well on."

This was true. We paid our rent, groceries, all living expenses, and we saved seventy-five dollars a month.

Then came the Depression. We were fortunate because he was never laid off from the Great Southern—nor was his salary cut. Consequently we were not hurt, ourselves. Our friends envied us because many of them had to move in with their families to exist. When we bought a new Chevrolet and paid cash for it—$375.00—in 1929, they marveled at this and said, "Naide and Mac are rich." I felt guilty because the Depression had hit so many and caused hardships and suffering.

The good part about it was that we were able to help others in our family and friends financially.

My husband took five dollars to the grocery store each week. This gave us a generous amount to buy enough to last a whole week.

I remember one trip we took to Weingarten's on Saturday. At that time we still drove a Model T Coupe. We loaded the groceries on the ledge back of the seat. Mac had played golf in the morning and still had his golf bag lying on the ledge. When I got home, I was incensed because my Farmer Brown bacon was not in my groceries.

"Mac, honey, they did not give us my Farmer Brown bacon and we paid twenty-nine cents for it."

99

I called and said, "You did not give me my bacon."
They said, "Sorry, you did not leave it here."
About three months later my husband came home from playing golf and said, "I found our pound of Farmer Brown bacon. For months my clubs were very greasy. I could hardly play golf with them. So finally today I turned the golf bag upside down, shook it, and what came out but our pound of Farmer Brown bacon!" *(Unfinished at the time of her death.)*

"Naide" McDaniel and her husband "Mac" had two children, Guy and Lynn, born during the Depression. Over the years she engaged in numerous volunteer projects for her Episcopal church, the USO, her children's schools. She was an avid collector of antiques and inveterate decorator, who taught the elements of design to others who later became well-known Houston decorators. She took active part in creative groups for writers, artists, and stitchers and—with Mac—dancers. When Mac retired in 1965, the couple moved to the Conroe area. He died in 1970 after forty-two years of marriage. Meanwhile, Naide had organized another writers' group named for one of her writer sisters, Hughie Call, and had joined painters' and stitchery clubs. She remained engaged in all of her creative groups for the rest of her life, traveling to Austin on the day before she died to visit friends and have a picnic among the wildflowers. She was at work on her Depression memoir at the time of her death at age eighty-four. Her most memorable trait was her unflagging encouragement of the creative endeavors of her many friends.

(8) Zenaide and Mac McDaniel

Section II

Oklahoma
and the South

ROY L. FISH

Desperation

During the spring of 1988, I made a sentimental journey to Hastings, Oklahoma—the birthplace of my father (who died in 1986) and me. Dad (Henry Joseph Fish) was born in 1907, the year of statehood and five years after Hastings was founded. I came along in 1932, born in a room rented from Dad's parents. The Depression was deep and ravishing.

Hastings was but a scar on the rolling prairie, even in its heyday, but it had experienced a crescendo. Dad had told me about the Oklahoma National Bank, two newspapers, a brick kiln, and other businesses that died. Though a large lake was eventually developed several miles east of town, the place never recovered its former vitality.

My Great-Grandfather Daniel Fish died July 4, 1931, while visiting his eldest daughter "Ellie" in Clarendon, Texas. Only months before, he had nailed several new planks into his barn; Dad used those boards to make two trunks, the smaller one for my clothing. The other doubled as a dining table.

Uncle Ernest, a masonry contractor, later bought most of Hastings' brick buildings and used the brick on homes in Oklahoma City. Ironically, he seldom had a nickel to spend inside those buildings during his boyhood.

On my 1988 trip back to Hastings I visited the decrepit remains of my grandparents' home on the west side of town. As was common, the living room had also doubled as a bedroom, and slept too many to each bed. Six of Dad's siblings were still at home in 1937. Aunt Mamie was an endangered species among her five ruffian brothers. Hardly did she sweep the last room and straighten the meager furnishings than her brothers stampeded through like cattle, knocking furniture askew and leaving dirt or mud.

When those boys were nearly grown, I saw Grandma lash

105

them the length of the porch with a rope. Barefoot and in ragged overalls they ran, trying to dodge. Turned out to be beneficial training, for three of them would soon dodge bullets in war.

Grandpa quit farming. Merchants hired him to be night watchman. There was no police department. He toted a black-jack, a pistol, and a double-barrel 12-gauge shotgun.

As I looked through the rear kitchen door and into the "front" room, I recalled blackbirds flocking into the cedar tree just outside the front-room window. Uncle Leroy, being about fifteen, dashed into his parents' bedroom and ran back with the shotgun. He cocked both hammers on the fly, belly-flopped onto a bed and fired through the screen. Didn't kill anything but the screen. Not a feather floated to the ground, but flies buzzed through the screen's wounds. I wonder whether the ringing in my ears is due to medication for arthritis or the twin volleys of that big weapon half a century ago. Leroy had probably been influenced by the pulp western magazines which were either given to them or borrowed, for there was no money for books. Nor for newspapers.

Leonard, Ralph, and I trekked half a block to George Collins' home on Sunday mornings to read the "Katzenjammer Kids." We admired the "Kids'" mischief, and tried to emulate them. Too often we succeeded—or outdid them.

Just south of George Collins lived Mr. Martin, a retired railroad employee. He still carried his heavy gold railroad watch. Grandma did his washing and ironing for twenty-five cents. We kids delivered his laundry.

I stood at the north kitchen wall, where the long table flanked by two equally long benches served so long ago. Pinto beans and corn bread were the common fare every day. Potatoes were a rarity. Maxwell House coffee was for breakfast only. Despite Grandma's best efforts to civilize her sons, they dived upon the corn bread, grabbing and saying "dibs on the corner!"

Eventually, my grandparents exchanged their equity in their home for their debt to grocer Lon Bailey.

After reminiscing, I drove "uptown." A restaurant is located in the brick building where I used to purchase long, orange balloons for a penny each. A one thousand shot Red Ryder B-B gun, identical to the one I've owned for forty-seven years, rests over the kitchen door. Ancient newspaper articles, which had

106

only recently been found, were on the walls. One piece concerned a WPA project on which Dad worked; it was Hastings Lake for local water supply.

Most of the afternoon, I strolled throughout the cemetery. A strong wind whipped all day, reminding me of the ill winds of the Depression that tore the soul from Hastings.

Many left for California, abandoning their property rather than pay the paltry taxes. Uncle Tom bought two lots directly across from my grandparents for something like eight dollars. After he and his family lived on them in a tent for a little while, he sold them for several dollars' profit. To this day, those lots have never hosted any structure other than Uncle Tom's tent.

A fellow who married a Hooper—once neighbors near my grandparents' place—had the audacity to broadcast that he was going to Hollywood and get in the movies. That brash announcement about got him laughed out of town.

But it was no laughing matter when Clyde Barrow and Bonnie Parker came to town one Saturday. Grandpa recognized the notorious couple. The bandits could readily see that pickings were extremely poor; in any event, they left without bothering anyone.

Dad pulled cotton in season, and worked for the WPA when a job was available. Other times he walked the country offering to work for two days without pay, saying they could start paying him after that if they were satisfied with his work. But people simply didn't have money to hire anyone under any conditions.

Dad's brothers grew a garden behind the house. Two harnessed themselves to the push plow while the other guided it.

Those kids were often without shoes, even in wintertime. They quickly learned there was less pain if they dashed through snow and summer's goathead stickers to the outhouse.

The children pulled cotton, then enrolled in school after Christmas. This was their only chance to earn a little cash to hedge against leaner seasons. Sometimes they traveled to Arizona's cotton fields in a Ford Model T truck. As Uncle Ernest observed more than half a century later, they, like so many others, could have been the model family for the Joads in John Steinbeck's classic *The Grapes of Wrath*.

On at least two occasions, a Mrs. Jones hired my two young uncles and me to clean her chicken house for ten cents each. At five years of age, I was more in the way than help, but I received that wonderful dime. I have always considered it charity.

My sister Edna Mae was born in January, 1935.

Dad's brother Floyd somehow amassed fifteen cents and bought a goat. He traded the animal for a pack of Camels, which enabled him to break even.

Times remained tough. Several decided to try for employment in Monterey's sardine plants. Dad's uncle—also named Floyd—owned an old Chevrolet, but he couldn't drive anything but a bicycle. Dad agreed to drive them to California. Though only five years of age, I distinctly remember those hungry and hopeful Okies packed into the car—appropriately as sardines. The group, consisting of Uncle Floyd, his wife, Effie, and six-year-old daughter, Lenora "Snookie"; Uncle Willie and Aunt Eunice; Aunt Mamie (a teenager); and Dad set out for Amarillo and Highway 66 (America's Main Street) which led to the Promised Land.

Somewhere in the western desert, the owner of a repair shop offered to hire Dad to mechanic (something of which Dad had learned through necessity). He told Dad he charged fifty dollars (an exorbitant sum) to replace a water pump, and that people would pay it. Many streamed through, pursuing dreams of prosperity. They carried their sole possessions with them, which was invariably pitifully little—piled in, tied to, or stacked onto jalopies, giving rise to the unfunny joke that a rich Okie had two mattresses on top of his car. They would spend their last dollar to reach California and the jobs that surely awaited them. Dad desperately needed that job, but had agreed to drive to California and he kept his word. He always kept his word.

Dad described a tavern at Needles, California. Colorado River water was diverted over the tin roof to counter stifling heat; however, the interior boiled with activity. In Dad's words, "They were killin' ol' Tige." That old saying meant that the joint was jiving. The action must have been sufficiently boisterous to attract the attention of anyone in the vicinity, for I never knew him to enter a place that sold strong drink.

The situation at Monterey was grim. Fishermen were on strike for thirteen dollars per ton instead of eleven. The Fishes rented a hut near Cannery Row—the same place and era so vividly described by Steinbeck in his novel of the same name.

108

They gathered driftwood from the beach to cook with and scratched for employment.

Back home, we continued to live in Mr. Bull's two-room rent house (a common structure at the time) beside the railroad track.

Cousin D. L. Pettigrew came from Walters and stayed for a while. He made a slingshot and took me with him and killed frogs. Mama cooked their legs. Cousin had only one pair of overalls; he wore one of Mama's dresses while she washed them. That situation wasn't uncommon. Grandma Fish owned only two dresses—and both must have been near identical, for in my every remembrance of her she wore a drab and faded brown dress.

Finally, we went to stay with Mama's parents, John and Nancy Thompson, on Tom Kennard's place north of Randlett and west of Walters; according to my calculations, that was twenty-five to thirty miles from Hastings.

One day, Mama, Aunt Ella, Edna, and I set out for home in our Ford Motel T coupe to fetch jars of home-canned food and the few chickens that we had left behind. The car died. It was out of gasoline, but we had no money to buy any—not even at ten cents per gallon. About forty-five years later, at my parents' home in Lindsay, Aunt Ella told how they "pushed their guts out" getting the car up one rolling hill after another, finally reaching Hastings.

Given the hard and hungry era, it was a wonder that our meager goods hadn't been stolen in our absence. In fact, there had been an attempted burglary one night when all of us were at home. Mama sold the chickens and bought gasoline for the return trip to the Thompsons.

Quite often, I asked when Daddy was coming home.

Lyman Ford, a remote relative by marriage, had become a mechanic for Mayfield Chevrolet in Lindsay. He got Dad a menial job there; but even a menial job was a precious job. Dad had been in Monterey for about two months when he received the postcard with the job offer, at $9.95 per week, from Mr. Mayfield. Dad was thrilled.

There was no choice but to hobo his way home. His uncle tried to dissuade him, saying that the trip was fraught with danger, that he would surely get bludgeoned.

Dad left Monterey with $1.50 with which to travel fifteen hundred miles. He also had a cigar box of lobster claws and seashells for me. (Tales of beautiful California and the ocean fascinated those of us who had never seen them. Mama often said she wanted to see California before she died. That wish was realized many times.)

Dad consulted the appropriate experts—railroad bums, and was advised to go to Stockton and hop a freight train the northeastern route into Oklahoma. He hitchhiked to Stockton, arriving about dusk. As trucks unloaded apples into boxcars, Dad hollowed a bed in a patch of weeds; it almost became his deathbed.

He filched and ate four apples, but peeled only two. The unpeeled ones, coated with insecticide, made him violently ill. He was certain he would die. Had he not peeled two, he surely would have. But by morning, he had recovered enough to move about. A train pulled up at sunup. Hobos hopped from it; they ate grapes, then moved on. Dad ate the few grapes they left.

Again, Dad asked hobos for advice. They told him to go to Los Angeles and catch a freight. But they warned him that he would probably be jailed because the train traveled much too fast to allow anyone to jump before entering the rail yard. He would certainly be killed if he tried. He said he wouldn't get caught.

Miraculously, he survived the leap. How he did that, keeping the cigar box intact, not to mention himself, remains a mystery. He said, "It's a wonder I didn't break my fool neck." But he walked in the wrong direction and the police picked him up. The officers questioned him, saying that transients had caused trouble in the area. Dad told them that he had jumped from the freight train. They didn't believe him, saying that it couldn't be done. When he foolishly insisted, they arrested him and took his fingerprints. Nothing except riding the train was found against him; therefore, he and other hobos were sentenced to thirty days in jail. Dad's heart sank with despair, for the job and his family depended upon his reaching home, still fifteen hundred miles distant. Then the judge suspended twenty-seven days. Even so, three days was sheer agony. One internee, a Negro, was eager to get out and eat the small piece of bacon wrapped in his bedroll. Upon being released, they were warned to stay off of trains.

Dad hitchhiked a short distance, then hopped a freight enroute to Albuquerque, New Mexico. Immigration officials boarded at Twin Oaks, near El Paso. Dad feared that he was

110

going to jail again; but the officials were looking for illegal Mexicans and didn't bother Dad or the other Anglo. The train arrived in Albuquerque about dawn. Railroad detectives "bulls" were numerous and active, diminishing chances of catching a train from there.

Dad walked to a farmhouse a short distance from the city and chopped wood in exchange for food. He hadn't worked for long when the lady of the house brought a big tray of food. She told him that many came begging but few were willing to work.

He rode a train to Amarillo. There, he and six or eight others tried to bum a ride from a gas station. An Army Air Corps truck came by, headed for Oklahoma City. The driver let everyone on except for Dad, saying there wasn't room! There was indeed room. Dad figured that maybe he was so indescribably filthy, the man didn't even want him riding in the rear. Needless to say, Dad was again distraught.

Another freight train took Dad to Wichita Falls, Texas. Being less than forty miles from home, he splurged thirty-five cents for a plate lunch, then set out on foot with thirty cents in his pocket.

Between Wichita Falls and Burkburnett, he swam in a very muddy pond near the highway—the first "bath" he had since leaving Monterey thirteen days previously. He said his filth made the water even muddier! Back on the road, a friend happened by and drove him to us at Mama's parents.

The ocean souvenirs were priceless to me. Marco Polo's home-town acquaintances could hardly have been more impressed with the treasures he brought from Xanadu. For years, I occasionally got the items out and ogled.

The next day we set out for Hastings, bought one gallon of gasoline, probably at "Cookie Town," the general store on the Lawton highway. As the old Ford did on the trip to retrieve our canned goods and chickens, it died for lack of fuel. The county road grader came along and gave us a gallon. Once in Hastings, someone financed a tank of gasoline. Dad left us with his parents and drove the eighty miles to Lindsay.

Fourteen days after leaving Monterey, Dad parked the Model T at Mayfield Chevrolet. Having traveled more than fifteen hundred miles on $1.50, the gift of one gallon of gasoline and a tank on credit, and perseverance born of desperation, he walked into the dealership and asked Marion Mayfield whether he still had the job.

He did.

And our fellow townsman who was ridiculed for avowing to get into movies?

He did.

For years, we paid ten and fifteen cents each to see him in B-Westerns. He wore a black hat, a cigar in his face, and bossed his gang from the office of his saloon. Practically every White Hat that chased villains through black and white flicks were targets for his thugs.

Finally, he traded his stogie and black hat for a job and a white apron in Miss Kitty's Long Branch Saloon in Dodge City, Kansas. Glenn Strange finished his career as "Sam" drawing warm beer for the good, the bad, and the ugly—Matt Dillon, Doc Adams, and Miss Kitty; rafts of riffraff, and Festus.

The teenage waitress who served me lunch in Hastings was amazed when I told her that she trod the same floor and streets as had the bartender in Gunsmoke—the world's most popular TV show.

Dad's job included everything lousy and cold and filthy a shop had to offer—washing and lubricating cars, sweeping, cleaning, and operating the wrecker at all hours. Given that many highways were dirt that quickly turned to mud, the work was demanding. At least sixty hours per week.

Within a week or two of Dad's employment, he and Lyman Ford borrowed a pickup truck from Mayfield's used car lot (a common practice), and moved us to Lindsay. Dad then sold our Model T for ten dollars, I think it was, and bought Mama a pair of shoes for her twenty-sixth birthday.

Dad didn't fare as well as Glenn, of course, but our standard of living gradually improved. There were other dark periods, but we overcame. We rented a screened porch, half of which had been converted into a crude room. Rent was five dollars monthly. Next we rented a room from an elderly couple on Highway 19; then we moved across the highway into a two-room house; it was there that we had our first Christmas in Lindsay. Santa brought a green stake wagon, fruit, candy, a doll, and a harmonica. The horse and guitar I wanted never arrived. Not enough room on the sleigh, I suppose.

Dad mailed fifty cents per week to pay off our grocery and gasoline indebtedness in Hastings. Christmas, paying debts, groceries, rent, and seeing Glenn Strange on Friday nights all came out of that magnificent salary of $9.95 per week.

In November 1938, my sister Jane was born, making three children to feed and clothe.

Mr. Mayfield, a bachelor and only about nine years older than Dad, called Dad "Hawkshaw" (the name of a cartoon detective) and taught him to be a fully-qualified mechanic. Dad became a top-producer; he was known throughout the area for his workmanship and honesty which diminished not for the remainder of his life. In 1945, Mr. Mayfield died of heart failure while sitting in the showroom; that was a terrible blow for all of us.

We moved into a two-room home on the east side of town. When I was in the fourth grade, we graduated from the succession of one and two-room dwelling places and moved across the street into a modest frame home of four rooms; it was a mansion to us. Several years later, we bought it and Dad built a bathroom. It was in that home that I grew into manhood. Today, the old place is in sad condition. Bushes and trees have overgrown it so that it is scarcely visible from the street. But I visit it every time I return. Rather than weep, I give thanks for its shelter and the love and guidance of my warm family that made the place glow during many of my formative years.

I still have my "baby" trunk. The cigar box that still held the souvenirs from the ocean, and survived intact the hazardous journey from Monterey, was stolen from the trunk in about 1961. Also taken were a twenty millimeter round, a fifty caliber machine gun round, a clip of M1 rifle ammunition, and a large bullet I found long ago at the site of an Indian/soldier fight near Lindsay; but the most meaningful souvenirs had long been imbedded in my heart. Nobody can steal those!

Tex Ritter, Gene Autry, Roy Rogers, Ken Maynard and others were my boyhood heroes. The "villainous" Glenn Strange turned good guy warmed my adult heart; but the real heroes, and heroines, whose battles with black-hat economics paralleled the tribulations of pioneers, were my parents and numerous others like them who brought their families through the scathing, brutal Depression.

Roy Fish was born in Hastings, Oklahoma, January 6, 1932. He grew up from age five in Lindsay, Oklahoma. He labored in cotton patch and oil patch: roustabout, pipeliner and roughneck. He became a stone mason, brick layer and real estate agent and is the author of several pieces of fiction and nonfiction. He finished high school in 1968 at age thirty-six and received an Associate Business degree from Alvin Community College, Texas with real estate credits in 1978. He attended UHCLC and Stephen F. Austin State University in Nacogdoches. He lived in Nacogdoches sixteen years then moved to San Antonio in 1996.

MARY WHITSON LANGLEY

Fay Days, Old Ways

The survival of the Great Depression in Fay, Oklahoma was aided by our special days. No matter how hard things got, we could always look forward to a celebration.

Of our special days, there was none so special as the first day of May. We would set out to make a fabulous May Day Basket. We gathered flowers from our abundant gardens, and put them together with a special treat. That night we would place our floral offering on a doorstep, knock loudly, yelling, "May Day, May Day", then we would run to hide. Giddy with joy, we were delighted to see the receiver's surprise.

Memorial Day—we called it Decoration Day—was a time of reunion and reminiscence. We honored those dear ones with floral wreathes we made of crepe paper and bouquets of fresh garden flowers. At noontime we picnicked and visited relatives and old friends.

The Medicine Show was a highlight of the summer. There was the Medicine Man who had knowledge about medicinal pills guaranteed to cure each and all our ills. He also sold specialized soap and waterless shampoo. Boxes of candy were bought by the ton—the tops were used as votes for a popular girl to be the queen of the Medicine Show.

On Trades Day busy farmers from all around would gather their wares and come into town with fresh garden produce, chickens, eggs, butter, cheese and kegs of molasses or corn syrup. They sold or traded their wares for things essential, then they joined in games of dominoes, checkers, horse shoes, dipping their snuff, chewing tobacco, spitting, whittling, whiling away the lazy hours waiting for the weekly drawing from the stores. Then they returned home where chores waited, to begin the ritual all over again.

Halloween was perhaps the most exciting day of the year.

Ghosts, ghouls and goblins were part of the scene. With costume parades and apple bobbing, the creatures of the night were all out hobnobbing. The younger children were in their beds dreaming of the days they would be "Big Goblins" and allowed to put the outhouses in a row in the middle of the main street. The problem was if anyone was in the house when you moved it. Which did happen a time or two.

The morning after, you would find tools and rusty implements of every kind on top of the stores and the school. One year there was even a horse and buggy.

What did we do on a hot summer night in Fay, Oklahoma when all the chores were done for the day, when there was no air-conditioning, no TV to watch, no Nintendos to play?

At the end of the days when our chores were done long after the sun had set, we would gather in groups to make our plan for an evening of fun. We might go for a marshmallow and wiener roast down at McDonald's Creek, or play games like Blind Man's Bluff, Red Rover and Crack the Whip. Then we would drop in a heap around the blazing campfire and tell ghost stories by the flickering firelight, shivering in delicious, delightful fright.

Sometimes there would be a quiet visit to a watermelon patch where no one was ever eager to catch us. Uncle Roscoe would give us all the melons we wanted, but it was more fun to swipe one.

We played a game of "Go Sheepie Go" with hidden clues for those in the know. We divided into two teams. One captain would hide his group and go back to the second group and give confusing directions as to where the first group was hidden. The captain would try to lead the group astray—calling out signals for close (Grandma's Garters) or far away (Charlie's Apples). When the group was far enough away he would yell, "Go-Sheepie Go." The team making it back to the base first, won.

We sometimes played marbles for keeps in the warm summer sand treasuring our very special taw, seeing who would be the king of the marbles that day. Or we could walk on stilts six feet tall, surveying our domain with kingly eyes, jousting as knights of old.

You could find us in the hay fields making fairy tunnels or sliding down giant stacks of sweet smelling hay, playing "Jack and Jill" or "King of the Heap."

116

A game of "Cops and Robbers" often ensued with stick horses and wooden guns, whose rubber bands had the bite of a hornet's sting. We would vie to see who would be the cocky "Hop-A-Long Cassidy" of the day. Our jail would be in the dusty old cotton gin. The cells were bins meant for snow white cotton—not a freckled faced criminal.

Sometimes we would play a rough game of "tin-can hockey" or we would choose up for the best baseball team. I was always the last to be chosen. In fact they fussed over who had to take me. I couldn't walk and chew gum at the same time. But I could always pick a book from the monthly book-mobile, find my favorite place high in the catalpa tree among the cool green leaves to become a princess, *Joan of Arc*, Meg of *Little Women*, *Ramona* or whatever else I would wanted to be.

We might slide down to the old tire swing and fly sky high as I listened to the cottonwoods sing.

Our life in Fay centered around the train depot. We never, never missed the train as it pulled into the station. There was that thrill of the train's haunting whistle, the powerful engines throbbing, and the bustle of the incoming passengers. We then would rush up the hill for the parceling out of the mail, eaves-dropping on friendly conversations to find out what exciting news we or others would receive.

Often we made trips to the local creek seeking poke salad or other greens to enhance our daily meal. We would go fishing with an old cane pole and occasionally some would skinny-dip in the nearby river.

Johnny Sober's luscious cherry trees were always a temp-tation. But he, an understanding farmer, would give red lipped urchins breezy rumble seat rides out over the countryside alive with ocean fields of waving wheat. Our lives couldn't be sweeter. We would stop at the Weiser store for a penny bag of candy then we would go to Scott's Drug next door and get a coke for a nickel more.

Each year a humble circus came to our town. It broke the summer doldrums and brought us cheer. The boys carried water by the ton for the aging elephant. They all wanted to impress the pretty Miss Gee Gee of the *low* flying trapeze, and they could get free tickets to the performances.

The splendid Gypsies came, too, with all their glamour and

117

mystery. Our mothers were always in a big dither, being sure their belongings and precious children would be swiped by the Gypsies. They brought in all their clothes off the line, and ordered us children to stay in. They didn't know we would sneak down the trails to seek their spells and hear their wild tales.

We dug our caves and buried our treasures. Huck and Tom couldn't hold a candle to us. We had our secret places for our private girl talks. We loved to take long lilac-scented walks out to the river bridge or we loved to walk the rails of the railroad track laying out pennies to be flattened by the huge steam engines of the daily train.

We often gathered at someone's home to play cards, make fudge and pop corn or have a taffy pull. We would eat until we would almost pop. Then we might go to another home for a sing-along, singing far into the night. Sometimes we would just sit out on the sidewalk and swing our legs as we let our "melodious" voices reach the stars in accompaniment to banjos and guitars.

On a really dark night we listened on our old battery-powered radio to "Innersanctum's Creaking Door" and we'd yell boisterously and shriek with horror. Or maybe we would listen to the "Shadow Knows" as we covered ourselves from head to toe. On hot summer nights we would sleep outside in our back yards with the stars and moon for light. Then we could really get into the ghost stories.

Saturday nights, in the middle of the main street, we scrambled for a special seat in front of an outdoor screen where we would watch a silent movie. But what kept us coming back week after week was the serial featuring our favorite hero, who always saved some damsel from sudden death at the hands of the awful, gruesome, fearful creature.

There was a tiny diesel power plant that ran after sundown until ten o'clock and on Mondays for washing. After ten the whole town's lights went off! We depended on kerosene lanterns, gas lights or candles.

At the end of a long day we would head back home to the smell of fresh hot baked bread, with homemade jam and fresh churned butter, thinking there was no better place under the sun; no better place to be than our tranquil, little community.

Mary Langley and her twin sister Marley were the youngest of thirteen children. They shared a 1946 Valedictorian scholarship to SWOSU. In 1993, she retired after teaching elementary school for thirty-six years. She wrote poetry in the third grade in Fay, but did not start writing it again until she retired and joined a writers group in Montgomery County, Texas where she now lives. She has won many awards for poetry and prose and has published *Fay Days / Old Ways: Reminiscences of Fay*. Besides writing, she paints, sculpts and works with stained glass. She chairs the children's ministry at the Methodist church in Montgomery and is vice president of the AARP group there.

(9) l to r - Twins, Marley Whitson
Mary Whitson Langley - 1934

BOB QUINN

I Remember

Shreveport, Louisiana:—the cool March breeze drifting through
the open window of the bedroom, the refreshing coolness brush-
ing across my face and awakening me as I lay sleeping in the
small room. It would still be dark; however, dawn was only
moments away and I knew I must soon get up and tend to my
chores. Chores consisted of feeding and watering the chickens,
milking the Jersey cow and staking her in a nearby field for the
day.

It was 1936, the midst of the great Depression. My father
was out of work as were so many men. This was an embarrass-
ment to him since he and my stepmother, Rellie, had only been
married for two years and she had become the sole provider for
our small family of four. I had just turned nine the previous
month and my older brother Don would be thirteen in October.

It had been only a year since my father and Rellie informed
my brother and me that her meager salary at the Southern Bell
Telephone Company would have to be supplemented with other
means. Rellie was raised on a small farm in central Louisiana
and her idea was to acquire a Jersey cow to provide milk and
chickens for eggs and meat.

My brother Don and I were excited at the prospect of the
family having our own animals; however, we did not realize the
extent of what our involvement was to be.

It was not long before, with instructions from Rellie, we
became not only adept at milking the cow, but expert in caring
for the chickens. Taking care of the chickens also included
selecting certain members of the flock for the dinner table.
Choosing the unlucky hen or fryer also included separating its
head from its body with an ax, or as Rellie would prefer, wringing
its neck. It was a task none of us relished, but one that we
accepted as necessary if we were to eat.

Since my father was out of work, Rellie convinced him to start a garden in the back yard. In spite of his city upbringing he thought this was a great idea and threw himself as well as Don and me into the task of digging and cultivating a twelve by twenty-four feet plot of ground. It was not long afterward that our efforts were rewarded with sprouting corn, squash, egg-plant, tomatoes, and string beans. I can still remember Rellie, on her days off, picking beans and placing them in her apron as she worked her way along the long row of vines.

Jersey cows are known for not only their abundance of milk but also for the percentage of cream per gallon. With more milk and cream than we could use, we were able to make our own butter. We would let the cream set up in a churn and when it was ready, agitate it with the pumping of a stick that protruded from its top. I don't recall the name of the "stick." I'm sure it must have been called something other than "stick." Anyway, you could tell when it was butter. Rellie taught all of us how to separate the butter from what was now buttermilk. She would then work the butter with a spoon until all of the remaining buttermilk had been squeezed out of it. After a proper amount of salt had been added, the butter was packed into a wooden butter press that held a one pound block of the yellow gold. We never lacked for butter or buttermilk. Somehow I never acquired a taste for buttermilk. It was too tart and sour for my liking.

With perishable goods it became necessary to have an ice-box. I saw one just the other day in an antique shop with the astronomical price of $475! Our ice-box stood about four feet tall and had a place in the bottom for block ice. There was a hole in the bottom of the box for the melted ice to drain into a pan sitting on the floor. It became my job to keep an eye on the pan so that it didn't overflow. It was everyone's job not to keep the ice-box door open any longer than necessary so the ice would not melt prematurely.

Getting the ice was an adventure in itself. I always enjoyed accompanying my father to the ice house. The man at the ice house would let us come into the storage room, where there were huge blocks of ice weighing one hundred pounds each. It was particularly nice inside the ice house in the summertime. When the huge door was opened, clouds of vapor whirled around my head and I would take big breaths of the cool air into my lungs.

BOB QUINN

We always bought a twenty-five pound block of ice. The ice man would wrap a brown cord around it that was strong enough to carry it without breaking. My father would place the ice block on the bumper of our Model A Ford. He didn't want to get the car wet inside. Getting the ice was always the last thing to do before heading home. In spite of our haste, the ice would melt and we would end up with about five pounds less than when we started. It was only after a suggestion from a neighbor that we brought newspaper to wrap the ice in so that our ice loss became minimal.

In the evening, when all the chores were done, my brother and I would lie on the floor in front of the Atwater Kent radio and listen to Jack Armstrong, the all American boy, and Sergeant Preston of the Yukon. At the end of each episode of Sergeant Preston, the mountie would say to his dog in a deep voice, "Come along King, this case is solved."

Later, in the evenings, my father and stepmother would sit and listen to Fibber McGee and Molly, Fred Allen, Eddie Cantor, and the Jack Benny show. Rochester, on Jack Benny's show, was one of my father's favorite characters. Of all the shows on the radio, my folks preferred the Lux Theater. Don and I preferred Gangbusters by Phillip H. Lord. I can still hear the police car sirens and recall the refrain of "Johnny" prefacing each episode of Gangbusters with his page, "Call for Phillip Moreeese."

Recreation was not confined only around the homestead. There was a small community known as Cedar Grove a few miles from our house. On certain Saturdays, the community leaders along with the business men, would sponsor boxing matches in a ring erected on a vacant lot on Main Street. A referee would stand in the middle of the ring and coax youngsters to put on the gloves and spar for the crowd. There were always willing takers. The prize, whether you won or lost your bout, was free tickets to the local cinema. I went up one night and ended up watching the movie with a bloody nose.

Occasionally, there would be a greased pig chase. A young pig, weighing no more than twenty-five or thirty pounds, was coated with axle grease and then released among a crowd of on-lookers. The person who could catch the squealing pig and manage to hold onto it became the pig's new owner. Quite a prize in those days.

There was a park at the edge of town with a cabin where the

123

Boy Scouts of America met. Also, there were a few tennis courts, which were rarely used for anything except for youngsters to roller skate. We would devise hockey sticks out of tree limbs and use tin cans for pucks. Someone always managed to go home with skinned knees or elbows.

During summer vacation, the civic association would erect a screen in the park and show a movie as well as a cartoon, just like at the theater. Everyone sat on the grass with umbrellas ready in case of rain. I was reminded of this when, in 1944, my Navy amphibious unit would sit on the ground after the invasion of Guam and watch movies in the same manner. We didn't have umbrellas, however; we had our ponchos in the event of rain which occurred more often than not.

Rellie always took her vacation from the telephone company during the school summer vacation. We would all go to Jena, a small town in central Louisiana where Rellie's parents and many of her siblings as well as cousins and aunts lived. When Rellie had to return to work, my brother and I were allowed to spend several weeks with her parents or at least as long as they could stand us.

We had a cousin named Bo who lived about a mile away. Everyone was about a mile away since the land surrounding the houses were acres of farmland. Bo, Don, and I would explore the woods and fish and swim in the abundance of creeks that criss-crossed the forests.

Every Saturday my grandfather hitched up his two mules to his wagon, loaded it with eggs and fresh vegetables, and took them into Jena to trade for staples such as flour, salt or whatever he could best bargain for. My grandmother always made sure he brought back material for her to make a dress or a shirt for Mr. Willis. That's what she always called my grandfather, Mr. Willis.

My grandmother called food, "vittles". I never ceased to be amazed at the simple but tasty fare or "vittles" she placed on the long wooden table in the old farmhouse. She was always the first to arise in the mornings. You could smell the wood burning in her stove and hear the clanking of the round iron cover that protected her pots from the fire.

Breakfast was a feast with eggs and bacon, potatoes, and hot biscuits with cream gravy. Lunch was light, served with an occasional piece of apple pie that had been stored in a "safe" located in the dining area. I saw one of these old safes in that same antique store with the ice-box. It also had a fancy price of $350. Supper (we called it supper instead of dinner) consisted of a glass of milk with cornbread crumbled in it. We were allowed to add sugar if we wanted.

In the corner of the dining area there was a clean number three galvanized bucket filled with water from the well located in the front yard. It was where milk was stored and kept cool since there was no ice to be had.

It was the same type of galvanized buckets that were stacked neatly next to an outbuilding where my grandmother did her weekly washing. The clothes were placed in a big iron pot filled with water. It sat on iron stakes over a fire that heated the water to almost a rolling boil.

Grandmother would punch and poke the clothes with a long stick before removing them and scrubbing each garment on a washboard. The galvanized tubs were filled with clean fresh water for rinsing before the clothes were wrung out by hand and finally hung on a clothes line to dry in the sun.

On Saturday mornings the tubs were filled with water and placed in the sun. By evening the water was warm and ready for each of us to take a bath. My brother and I usually shared the same bath water.

As I think now about the lifestyle of my grandparents I often wonder what they would think about today's modern conveniences. After all, there was very little time for anything in their lives except work and trying to subsist off the land. And yet they seemed perfectly happy. It is said "you never miss what you never had." I guess that is true. I never heard either grandparent wish for something they could not possibly have and doubt if they even knew certain modern conveniences even existed. Modern for the times, that is. Even Rellie had an electric washing machine with a wringer attachment that had electrically driven gears to turn the rollers.

Sunday was a day of worship. It was the day "the Lord intended for us to rest." So sayeth my grandfather. No one was allowed to work, play, hunt or fish on Sunday. Grandfather would sit on the front porch in one of the chairs he had made and just gaze out at his acreage. I wonder now what he was thinking

125

(10) Bob Quinn in front of the Paramount Drive-In owned by his father

during these moments. I would guess he was giving thanks to the Lord for his land and his way of life.

It was a good feeling to get back home again. School would start on Tuesday, the day after Labor Day. Don was in high school and he had only to walk three blocks to catch the school bus. I was not so fortunate. There was no school bus for grade school, and after my chores were completed, I would walk the three and half miles to Atkins Avenue Elementary school. I don't remember it being a hardship, even when it was cold, windy, or raining. As I said, "You don't miss what you never had."

As it turns out, we were more fortunate than many in our semi-rural neighborhood. There were some families with pre-school children, leaving the mothers home-bound to care for their youngsters. The men in these families would leave for another part of the country, in the hopes and sometimes promise of finding work. Some joined the Civilian Conservation Corps or the CCC as it was more commonly known. The CCC was one of the New Deal programs of President Franklin Roosevelt and was not only beneficial in providing employment to thousands of unemployed men, but in later years rewarded this country with vast forests.

It has been over sixty years now. Yet there are times when certain events will jog an incident kept safe for so long in my memory's space bank. Only yesterday I purchased a reel type push lawnmower, prompting me to recall these events of yester-year. I could have had a power driven gas mower, but as nice as they are, the old push mower was the more practical purchase for my small yard.

I hear some of my peers wistfully wishing for the "good old days." My first inclination is to remonstrate with them. Would they be willing to give up their television sets, their expensive automobiles, the ability to fly across this great nation coast to coast in just four hours? Would they miss the morning newspaper that is delivered to their front door?

Or on the other hand, would they miss reading about the drive-by shootings that occurred the night before—or the rape of a young girl or woman who has been left for dead on the side of a remote highway—or miss worrying about their child being abducted while playing in their front yard and being molested or murdered? Would they miss reading of the drug driven crimes

127

and the appeal for funds to build more prisons?

All of this is just a part of modern America. Many say they would trade it all for the simple life of yesteryear. They would enjoy reading by the light of a kerosene lamp and getting up wintry mornings in a cold room. They wouldn't mind going to an outhouse in the middle of the night or on a cold blustery day. They wouldn't even miss the morning paper that is delivered to the front door.

How about you? Which would you choose?

In February 1942, shortly before his fifteenth birthday, Robert Neal (Bob) Quinn left his home in Shreveport, Louisiana. He traveled through the southwest where he performed odd jobs and met many "MAD HATTER" characters along the way. In 1943, at sixteen, he altered his birth certificate and joined the U.S. Navy. Bob served aboard a ship in the south Pacific and participated in several island invasions and sea battles. He witnessed the signing of the Japanese unconditional surrender aboard the U.S.S. Missouri on September 2, 1945 in Tokyo Bay. After the war Bob spent four years with the Navy at Guantanamo Bay, Cuba. In 1952 he was employed by IBM in Shreveport, Louisiana. He retired from IBM in 1983 and is now retired in Montgomery, Texas. Bob's interests are landscape painting, writing and golf.

THERESA WESTCOTT
Rhea Flynt Story

Rhea Remembers

December 22, 1935, when most families were preparing for the Christmas holidays, Rhea G. Flynt put her four-year-old son on a night train bound for Florida. Louis, or "Wiggles" as he was called, had rheumatic fever and was not expected to live. His Aunt Chic traveled with him since she was a nurse. When the doctors advised that he would not recover in the cold, wet winter of Rochester, New York, Rhea did the only thing she could: send him to a warmer climate. As he boarded the train that night, Wiggles could barely walk.

The next morning Rhea packed up her eleven-month-old daughter, Betty Janine, along with the housekeeper and housekeeper's little boy, and headed for Florida by car.

This was just another in a string of events proving to Rhea that in times of need, you do what you have to do. Janine, born five weeks premature, had been in an incubator for some time. Rhea was still recovering from a phlebitis that had developed during her pregnancy and which left her bedridden for six months after the birth. Eventually she was able to get up on crutches and start caring for her baby, but her leg was black and not responding to treatment. Her own life was in question.

Now, with the baby eleven months old and Louis already on the train, Rhea headed South. Her husband stayed in Rochester where he had a dependable job at Eastman Kodak. He agreed to send her fifteen dollars a week.

Rhea's father-in-law drove them as far as Washington D.C., thinking that there would be no snow on the roads south of that and that she should have no trouble the rest of the way. That particular winter, however, the winter of 1935-36, there was snow and ice as far south as southern Georgia.

On their own, a few miles outside of Washington, the women had a flat tire. Rhea hitch-hiked in the bitter cold to buy

129

a tire and find someone who would change it for her. It took a good part of the afternoon, since all of their luggage was strapped on top of the spare. When they finally started out again, they were cold and hungry and the baby was crying.

For five days on the road they battled the blizzard. Each morning they had to wait until the ice was cleared from the highway before they could get started. Some afternoons they stopped as early as three o'clock because so much snow covered the roads and visibility was near zero.

Christmas came and went on this miserable journey as Rhea and her companions slowly worked their way South to get to four-year-old Louis in Florida.

The plan was for Aunt Chic to take Louis to Miami and find a place to live. Then she would send a letter to St. Augustine for Rhea to pick up. Never having been south of Washington before, Rhea was depending on maps and instincts. This made the news heartbreaking when she received Aunt Chic's letter saying that children were not allowed in the apartment houses and therefore they had no place to live.

Another night on the road would bring them to the Ft. Lauderdale Hotel where they were to meet Louis and Aunt Chic. There, Rhea would have to do some serious thinking about how to provide for her family.

A glimmer of hope sparked her spirit as she pulled up to the hotel and saw her son Louis running toward her. He had improved tremendously in just five days and his fever was gone. Yes, she thought, everything was going to work out, one way or another.

Looking for a place to call home, they discovered that they could not even rent a trailer with three children. Their search led them to one dead end after another, until that Saturday, when they drove into Ollie Trout's Trailer Park in Miami. The salesman wanted to sell them a trailer, but that was out of the question since they had no funds. Desperate by now, Rhea agreed to look at a small homemade twelve-foot trailer costing $225. Rhea explained that she couldn't get cash from Rochester until Monday. An insistent seller agreed to let them move in immediately with a very small deposit of ten dollars.

Rhea, Aunt Chic and the housekeeper (who remains unnamed in Rhea's memoirs) pooled their money to come up with the deposit. They were left with less than five dollars between them to last until Monday. With it they bought five tin spoons, five tin pie plates, five tin cups, milk, and bread. They had linens and bedding in the car, and the seller agreed to leave the gasoline stove in the trailer along with a skillet and a pot.

On Monday Rhea sent a wire to her husband requesting the $225 as well as the fifteen dollar weekly payment that had been agreed upon. He had to get a loan against the car, but the money arrived and the deal was closed that day. Rhea found herself the proud owner of a trailer. It had two double built-in beds, and the space between them was just big enough to put the baby's little portable bed, as long as everyone else was in bed first. Aunt Chic slept in the car. The weather was beautiful, so they did all of their living outside and used the trailer primarily for sleeping.

The housekeeper and her son stayed until February. After that, Aunt Chic had her bed. Aunt Chic, however, could not obtain a nurse's position in Florida because they would not accept her out-of-state license.

Then, an unexpected twist of fate. Ollie Trout, owner of the trailer park, needed help with his taxes. This was something Rhea could do.

Rhea was the only child in her family to receive an education. She gained the privilege by solving a puzzle in the newspaper which awarded her free tuition in a business college in Syracuse, New York. So, at the age of fourteen, she had quit high school to attend college.

Rhea was no stranger to the work force. After college she worked as a stenographer in many different offices, each one paying a little better than the one before. As a live-in secretary for Senator Gates, she was faring better than the rest of her family and often used her money to buy or make dresses for her three younger sisters.

At one time Rhea worked at a new store that opened up in town - Woolworth's. She also worked in the Herbert Hoover Campaign raising funds for starving children. Her salary was eighteen dollars a week. When the campaign needed some immediate help to get out literature, they had paid five dollars per hour for envelope stuffers. Her three younger sisters, a set of twelve year old twins and a ten year old, began making more money than Rhea. When the campaign was over, she had gone to work in the U.S. Ordnance Department as secretary to a lieutenant and a major in the First World War.

By 1918 Rhea was working in a brokerage firm and from there she had several other secretarial jobs, gaining experience and knowledge. At the age of twenty-nine, she had married and settled down to have children.

There was no doubt about it. If there was bookwork to be done, Rhea knew how to do it. With such a long resume for her thirty-six years, Rhea dressed in white linen shorts and matching jacket, a rubber stocking from the knee down and, still limping from her phlebitis, went to see Ollie Trout. She got the job. Now she was not only the owner of her very own trailer, but she was a woman employed-in 1936. She got her trailer space rent-free and near the office, meals with eighteen other employees, and six dollars a week in cash. Things were looking up.

In early May, Rhea took her children and her belongings and headed back to Rochester, New York. The tires on her trailer were worn smooth and although she was advised not to leave the trailer park on them, new tires were not in the budget. She took a chance and a prayer and made it home safely.

Three months later, Louis was sick again. Serious bronchitis shot his temperature up to 104 and Rhea was told it would have to be another winter in Miami. They had traded the trailer for an eighteen-foot modern one with a refrigerator and breakfast room. In September Rhea drove, pulling the eighteen footer, back to Ollie Trout's. She was on her own this time, since Aunt Chic had moved to New York City.

Back in Miami, Rhea was welcomed with open arms. She got her job back, meals for herself and her children and a raise in pay. Ollie Trout had put up a playground for the kids and installed a voycall on Rhea's desk so that she could talk to them any time, anywhere in the park.

Every day at five, Rhea would use her voycall to tell her children it was shower time. Louis (Wiggles) led his two-year-old sister to the trailer, adjusted the shower water and made sure she washed with soap. Then he took his own shower. Both the children would come over to the restaurant for dinner with their clothes on but their bodies still wet and their hair still dripping. The other restaurant guests always told them how nice they looked and complimented Janine on how well she combed her own hair.

For five years Rhea made the trip back and forth, leaving Rochester in September, in time for school in Miami, and going north again when school was out. Every year Wiggles got sick in the month of August with high temperatures but recovered well in the balmy weather of Florida.

Finally, Rhea decided to stay in Miami. She had many opportunities at Ollie Trout's Trailer Park. He expanded to include a grocery store, a meat market, bingo games, a barber shop and a beauty parlor. The late Depression years were good to Ollie Trout. Rhea's job was to oversee all of these and the many new employees who came in. She was also a Notary Public, a public stenographer, and in charge of the teletype on a fifty-fifty basis.

With her salaries she was able to build a home - a duplex. Since her husband, still in New York, would not sign for a loan for this house (he was quite conservative with money in the 1930's), she told the finance company that she was divorced. They gave her credit.

Once she had established that, she could make other purchases as opportunities arose. At one time she owned four trailers which she rented during the season for twenty-five dollars a week. Then she sold them at a big profit to folks who were leaving Miami.

Rhea Flynt became a successful businesswoman. A woman ahead of her time, she was independent, gutsy, and not afraid to take chances. She bought one-quarter interest in the Kawai Music Store where six music instructors gave lessons. She held on to this venture for many years, during which her children, Louis and Betty, became musically accomplished.

Throughout her life, Rhea has been a go-getter, never letting an adventure or an opportunity slip by. Being a woman was no deterrent to her as she advanced her career in the 1920's and '30s; in fact, it was her maternal love and the need to provide for her children that urged her onward despite danger and uncertainty. She was a good caretaker, raising her children on her own at a time when this wasn't common.

Now, at the age of ninety-four, she lives in Jacksonville, Florida with her daughter. Her eyesight is very poor and so is her hearing. But age did not take her determined spirit and her sense of adventure. She laughs as she recalls for me the one thing in her life that frightened her. In 1928, when she was twenty nine years old, there was a pilot offering airplane rides in a field near her home; fifteen dollars for five minutes. Always one to seize the day, Rhea hopped right in. The engines were roaring and the pilot with his cap on didn't notice that when Rhea closed the door, it came off its hinges. She tried to tell him, but when he took off anyway, it was all she could do to hold on. For five minutes he flew her around the sky with her leg dangling out the doorway and her hair blowing wildly. When they landed and she stepped out looking as if she had seen a ghost, no one else wanted a ride. He didn't even give her money back! It was over fifty years before Rhea got on another airplane. In 1982, I met her in Florida and we flew together to Rochester, New York to visit Louis, my father.

I am proud to call you Grandma, Rhea. I would like to think that some of your independence and determination have been passed on to me. When my children are old enough, they will hear your story and they will be taught what strength of spirit lies within their roots.

Rhea G. Flynt remained an independent woman throughout her lifetime living in her own apartment despite many physical problems. At the age of seventy-six she became caretaker of her youngest grandson, David Sumpter, whom she raised through his teenage years. When her health failed her, she lived with her daughter, Betty, until she passed away on March 8, 1994 at the age of ninety-four. Her ashes were laid to rest by Louis, her son, in a retreat campground in Florida, where she had often spent weekends with her daughter. Louis recalls that when he left home at the age of nineteen, she was sad, but encouraged him to better himself by seeking employment in New York. "She must have been pretty sure she had done a good job."

BECKY SANFORD

My Auspicious Entry Into the Workforce

I was an English major in my first degree at Blue Mountain College (Mississippi) and was eagerly trying to find a high school in need of my English teacher training, when, in my senior year, the Great Depression of 1929 crashed upon this country. All such jobs were quickly given to families and friends of school boards. My favorite English professor called me to his office when I was despondent over my prospects and told me that the Memphis Public Library was planning to give a qualifying examination in order to assemble an apprentice class in library work, which, if successfully completed, would entitle one to a job in the city library system.

"On your way to your home in Mississippi, just go into the Memphis Library and take the exam," said my professor. "You'll probably pass the tests."

I had no earthly idea what library work might be because I had never lasted more than five minutes in the college library before being thrown out by the librarian, who was the president's mother. It was really not a case of my having made any noise, but I would always enter the door, silently impersonating some faculty or student character, and this would cause an instant explosion of laughter among the readers. Such frivolity was a strange and ironical background for my entry into a scholarly profession to which I would belong for the first twenty years of my working life.

In order to travel from Blue Mountain in extreme Northeastern to Coldwater in Northwestern Mississippi (a fairly short distance) in those days, it was necessary to take two railroad lines and change trains in Memphis, Tennessee. Accordingly, between trains, I ran (literally) to the Memphis Library from the depot—about two miles. The Head of Circulation gave the examination on which I made a grade of ninety-eight, having answered that Lebanon was in Palestine! (In 1952, I was in Lebanon on my way to a secret propaganda conference on Cyprus Island.)

There were only four women and no men in the apprentice class. Besides myself, only one person had any college credits. Grace Flournoy had finished two years at a Presbyterian college. Two high school graduates were said to have been accepted because of their "nice" personalities. Willie Bamberger was truly a sunbeam, but Shirley Jones was "cold grits." Shirley talked with upper and lower teeth locked together and never smiled. Our first and only exchange of communications was as follows: "Shirley, since there are only three lockers for four people, would you like to share one with me?"

Said Shirley, "How do I know that you wouldn't take money out of my purse?"

Shirley and Willie both married without having set off any literary bonfires, and Grace and I later became roommates at various boarding houses until she married. Initially, we were both assigned to the largest of the branch libraries, where there was also a young man who had just finished college.

We apprentices were compelled to spend our first three months of training without pay, at the end of which we were paid fifty dollars per month. At the end of six months, our pay was raised to sixty-five dollars per month. Our colleague, Duke Moody, with no training nor experience, had entered at ninety dollars per month!

After two years, I was promoted to head of North Memphis Branch Library at a salary of seventy-five dollars per month. I was also lewdly a bloody capitalist, for my cousin was teaching high school English for forty dollars per month. I held this position for three years, during which, through extensive publicity, I managed to increase the book circulation from the lowest of the branches to second place. This was surpassed only by that of the largest branch which would always be in first place due to demographic situations; namely, a density of a highly literate population of doctors, lawyers, engineers, and the like. All of my publicity work was done on my own time for there was never but one person on duty at my branch at one time.

Meanwhile, although President Roosevelt with his "New Deal" had managed to get the bread lines off the streets, a woman who had a job was subject to the chilling fear that she might very well be holding the last job in the whole world. Whatever ignominy or injustice was dealt to her in those days had to be endured, for the only mobility available was straight down. There is an old British nursery rhyme which reads, "Hold tightly to the hand of nurse, in case of meeting something worse!"

I was constantly kept aware that although I was being allowed to hold a very responsible position, I was technically, nevertheless, an untrained librarian without a Library School degree because any other degree was only the basic requisite for entry to the professional school.

One could qualify for a library degree by completing four summers in a professional school. This was my only possibility. Accordingly, my uncle signed a bank note for me so that I might borrow two hundred fifty dollars for my first summer at the University of Illinois. Toward the end of the summer, a faculty member offered me a three-quarter time job in the library so that I might return for the fall semester, continuing straight through until graduation—and for the magic sum of seventy-five dollars per month. This was exactly what I was being paid to run the North Memphis Branch Library!

I returned to my Memphis job and obtained permission (verbal, of course) to be absent without pay for eighteen months. Before I left, however, the Head Librarian called me to his office to tell me that he had "great advancements for you upon your return; something really worth your while!"

By the time I graduated, I had already processed for a full-time staff job at Illinois University Library and had been accepted for graduate school. Having secured this "beach head," I thought that I would merely touch base with the Head of Memphis Public Library to see what "really worth while" he had in mind for me. He replied by letter that: "We are sorry that at present, we really have nothing in mind for you; but if you should find a job elsewhere first, and later bring that experience with you, we might be able to place you somewhere in the system."

I ignored replying to this letter, and two weeks later, the follow-up arrived. "By considerable shifting of personnel, we are now able to offer you a position at ninety dollars a month."

In my young days, I was not capable of laying the appropriate body language on such people as that librarian, but now, so many years later, I no longer have this deficiency; so Mr. "C", wherever you are, even if there are ladies present, take your splendid offer and shove it!

Meanwhile, back in Memphis, remember Duke Moody, who was making ninety dollars per month, even during my starving apprentice days!

Thus was my introduction to the status of women in the working world. Forty years later, the ending was strangely similar to the beginning.

At Illinois, all of the library jobs were under state civil service. I was in charge of a room containing all reserved reading for History, Political Science, French, German, Spanish, and Italian. The room was one-and-a-half times the size of the football field. The Head of the Circulation Branch was Miss Windlow, who had graduated from library school in the year of my birth, and had never worked anywhere else. I used to think that she might well have been a good cataloguer, because of her aptitude for instant classification of her assistants. Every southern accent came from the mouth of a lazy person. If that mouth belonged to a male, Miss Windlow would bash him for awhile, but he could improve his lot by marrying—preferably with a girl from north of the Mason-Dixon line. Should this partially literate male and wife produce a baby, then Miss Windlow would forgive him his geography and would soon find a way to give him a pay raise, even if his duties were on a level equivalent to those of a young teenage "page boy" in a public library.

As a southern female, one had a much less rosy prospect of basking in the warmth of Miss Windlow's approval. She had come in lazy, and she would leave lazy.

I worked so fast and with such singleness of heart that I never stopped to tie my shoe for six years; yet, Miss Windlow never let me out of her dog house—not even on a leash.

Three years later, when I returned for a visit from my position as Post Librarian at West Point's Basic-Advanced flying School and wearing a decoration on my uniform pocket, Miss Windlow smiled at me benignly and said, "Miss Sanford, in all of your six years in my department, I never once saw a wrinkle in your skirt." (Librarians did not use given names casually in those days, especially if there was an age span or a rank span intervening.)

"Well, Miss Windlow, one has to sit down in order to wrinkle a skirt. The fact is, you used to get yours 'rump sprung.'"

The men were not scheduled on Saturday afternoons and could go to the football games. I was always kept on Saturday duty, so that now, even at the age of eighty-eight, I would not know a "first down" from a jock strap!

In the early years of American Librarianship, women held a majority of all positions because they were in the majority of personnel in that profession. It was socially and intellectually acceptable long before American women dared to put a tentative foot into such wild and raucous areas as medicine, engineering, law, etc. Accordingly, with a few exceptions, the University of Illinois Library executive jobs were held by youngish middle-aged women, who would hold these jobs until retirement or death. In the event of either, young men would replace them.

Therefore, when a woman on a working fellowship finished her Master's degree, she knew very well that she must move on or reconcile herself to living in a "no progress" situation. So in the mood of Scarlet O'Hara's decision, I thought, "Tomorrow, God, tomorrow I'll concentrate on my future, but now I'll do something more interesting, such as visiting New York City for the first time." I honestly believed myself to be the only living person who had never been to New York!

A nun friend of mine, who was on duty at the Convent of Our Lady of the Cenacle on Riverside Drive, had already invited me to stay at the Convent should I come to New York; otherwise, I could not have made the trip.

On my first trip "downtown" to look about, I found myself needing a ladies' room just as I was in the vicinity of the New York Public Library at Fifth Avenue and Forty-Second Street. Of course, that would be a quick solution; so, in I went, although I had made no plans to visit there. Once in, I decided to have a quick look around. A very pleasant middle-aged librarian with magnolia petals dripping from her accent asked me if I needed help. I introduced myself, and she immediately urged me to apply for the staff, saying that not one person in Central Circulation had a Master's Degree. She took me to the Chief, who was a lady with a sort of angel face and soft manners and who also encouraged me to take a job there at once. I knew that it was quite salutary to show on your resume that you had worked at

New York Public Library, even if the salary was no better than your present one.

I was afraid to cut my strings at Illinois, for I truly loved academic life and academic people; so I offered to work without fee for the month of my vacation in order to sample the situation. Needless to say, the royal red carpet was rolled out for me, but as soon as the umbilical cord with Illinois was severed, the New Yorkers moved in on me with such rudeness that my very soul was blighted. It was unbelievable to me, for I had grown up in a world of gentle manners, and politeness was a way of life. I was not experienced in combating such conduct, but I should have followed the advice of my nun friend who said, "Becky, the very next time anyone says something rude to you, answer sharply, 'You go to Hell!' that person will be more careful in addressing you afterward!" How right you were, Mother O'Connell, but I preferred to look for an escape to a better world.

The Department Head with the angel-face turned out to be such a ferocious dragon that she yelled at a page boy one day and caused him to wet his pants before he could get out of sight!

There were no men in Central Circulation, for they were dug in snugly in Reference or Ordering.

In the fourteen purgatorial months at New York Public Library, during which time World War II had been declared early in my second month, I can honestly say that I did not have one professional experience of any value. I learned one geographical fact, however. Don't look for Bryant Park on the city map because the library is sitting in it!

As a life experience, however, some days were sprinkled with happenings which brightened the dreary vista.

People with hilarious names, having been to court and had them legally changed, would come in dutifully to have their library cards rewritten. Michael Archangel had become Michael Arch; Arthur Bastard became A. Bast, for example.

Saturdays were my favorites, for they were always good for a couple of purse snatchings to break the monotony. One glorious Saturday, we had three snatchings and one man urinating on the books in the Philosophy section. Spinoza and Kant were especially soaked.

As Hitler's persecutions grew and spread to many European nations, wealthy refugees came piling into the library. One day, a young inconspicuous looking man applied for a library card. He wrote his, "Felix, Arch-Duke of Austria." Said the Library assistant, "What is your surname?"

Said he, "Madame, I am Felix, Arch-Duke of Austria."

Said she, louder and shriller than before, "You can't have a library card if you don't have a last name because that is how we alphabetize the cards!"

After she had crucified His Royal Highness, some members of the public shouted, "For crying into the beer, lady, put down Hapsburg for his surname!"

In my fourteenth month of torture, I was transferred to the Harlem Branch. On my first day there in that black world, I was trying to help a little girl fill out an application. She said to me, "Don't try to tell me how to run my business!"

My escape was close at hand.

The U. S. Military Academy at West Point needed a professional librarian to establish and supervise the Post Library at its new Basic-Advanced Flying School, which was being built over the mountain from the Academy. The job had been offered to the only librarian in New York who had been kind to me. She was the sister-in-law of the Colonel in Command of the Ground School, and she recommended me because she did not want to leave Manhattan to which port her Marine husband would be coming on some weekends. Thus I was accepted for the job by the military, but that's another story.

Becky Sanford was born in Memphis Tennessee on March 23, 1910 and was reared in Coldwater, Mississippi—mother's ancestral home. She received an AB, Blue Mountain College; BS and MA, University of Illinois; Ph.D. Studies, Friedrich Alexander Universitaet (Erlangen, Germany). She was a professional librarian from 1930 to 1950 in Memphis, University of Illinois, New York City, West Point Flight School, Paris, France; Wiesbaden, Bremen, Bremerhaven, Nuernberg, Munich, Erlangen, Germany; Nancy, France; Liege, Belgium; Neimegen, Holland; Luxembourg. From 1950 to 1970, she was a film executive in U.S. Information Agency (federal government's official world-wide information program in 108 foreign countries). She was based in D.C., but traveled abroad on duty. Retired from government 1970, she wrote a by-lined column for Delaware Coast Press 1972-1973 and was media specialist for Holy Name School (Florida) 1982-83. Among her honors, she was decorated by U.S. Army 1944; by French Government, 1947 with its highest academic honor, Officier d'Academie. Winner in Delaware Bicentennial Writers Competition, and an award in Hollywood World Songwriters Competition, 1977. "First Lady of the Year Award" in Delaware, 1973. She is currently engaged in a work in progress an autobiographical collection of personal essays.

SANDRA J. COX
Charlie Lewis

Compassion in the Deep South

Because I was not born when the Depression began and I wanted to get a first-hand account, I asked my friend and neighbor Charlie Lewis for an interview. As my first question will indicate, I thought the Depression began at the moment the stock market crashed.

Charlie, tell me what the Great Depression was like in Natchez, Mississippi in 1929.

The people of Natchez didn't really know that the Crash would begin a Depression. The Crash didn't affect the price of cotton very much or the price of beans or anything else. The market didn't take any precipitous drop. It was later that the full impact of the stock market Crash began to sink in nationwide and over the whole world and the Depression—the real Depression—began to blanket the nation.

In 1927, two years before the Depression officially began, the Mississippi River had flooded and the economy of Natchez had been jolted. The two little towns of Vidalia and Perry had been absolutely wiped out. There was not a house that was not under water by ten-twelve feet and stayed under water for weeks. There was no welfare. They had no income. They lost all their savings. They were destitute.

If you're familiar with Natchez, you know it's on the bluff side of the Mississippi River. The plantation owners lived in Natchez but they had their farms across the river in Louisiana. After the big flood they began to rebuild, and a lot of them borrowed money. When the Crash came in 1929, it absolutely destroyed the economy of Natchez and those little towns across the river too. As the noose began to tighten, first one business would close then another and then another. Farming, as such, to raise a cash crop like cotton, corn and cattle, became the first victim. After a while people got to the point where they didn't have any money to pay their work hands or to buy fertilizer, so they grew what they could afford to till and take care of themselves, which was primarily a garden, and they raised their own livestock for their own slaughter.

Was your father a plantation owner?

No. He ran a store across the river and of course the store was wiped out and all the merchandise gone with the flood, so there he was without a store and without a job. But he wasn't any worse off than everybody else around...Later he operated another store, but as the great Depression spread across our land and one business after another closed, my father's store closed too. He went through hell, as most of his contemporaries did, and he just did whatever he could do to keep body and soul together. That's kinda where I remember the Depression really starting. I was twelve years old at that time—old enough to know what it was like.

Were you old enough to help too?

Yes, in the summertime, I would go to north Louisiana, where all my relatives were agrarian people, and live on a farm up there and raise food for all the family. I loved being there, but there was plenty of work to be done.

Did you see a lot of hobos and hunger during the Depression?

A lot of trains came through carrying many hobos going God knows where, but I didn't see anyone go hungry. People were very kind in those days. If there was a family in desperate need, people would take them clothes and food. People were far more compassionate then than they are today, and the church was very good.

Was it a Baptist church?

We had only one church house and the Methodists and Baptists shared it. I don't know what arrangements they had, but it seemed to work. Now the Negroes on the other hand, had three church houses. They had a Baptist, a Methodist and a Pentecostal, and the Pentecostal was by far the most popular and influential.

Charlie, how did the people recover without jobs and cash?

The only place to earn cash was at the sawmill. The sawmill was doing a fairly good business because everybody was rebuilding in that immediate vicinity. The money came from somewhere but I don't know where. Anyway, if you wanted a job to get

144

SANDRA J. COX

some cash money, you worked at a sawmill and that was about
it—a sawmill or a bank—but the sawmill generated the outside
income. That was the environment in which I lived from age
eleven to seventeen.

Hoover was the president when the Depression hit and he
was succeeded by Roosevelt. One of the first things Roosevelt did
was start the Civilian Conservation Corp, better know as the
CCC.

Now, I played a lot of tennis, and a tennis partner of mine
who was a few years older had already gone off to college. He was
getting a degree in Forestry and he told me, "Charlie, if you
haven't made up your mind what you're going to do, you better
give this some thought because everyone that graduates with a
degree in Forestry automatically gets a job."

I told him I wanted to study journalism.

And he said, "You can study journalism if you want, but if
you go to the *Natchez Democrat* you'll sweep that place out for
five years before you ever get a chance to write and then you can't
make anything."

So that's what sent me in that direction to study Forestry.

*Was the year you went on to college the same year the
Depression ended?*

Oh heavens no. The Depression went on for many more
years...When I finished high school in 1933, I didn't have any
money to go to college. Nobody did. So I went to work cutting
grass at a cemetery for fifteen cents an hour. I worked nine hours
a day, six days a week. I did that for a couple of years and saved
up enough money to see me through the first semester of college.

When I got to Mississippi State I began to look around and
find whatever work I could there. I swept the dormitories, waited
tables and delivered papers. I did anything that would generate
a little cash.

*Did the state of Mississippi reduce the tuition or anything
else to encourage education during that time?*

Mississippi was a poor state and about ninety percent of the
students were in the same shape I was in. Fortunately, it didn't
cost very much to go to school in those days. Mississippi has
always tried to make it possible for most people to get an
education. At one time Natchez had more millionaires per capita
than New York City and was a source of tremendous wealth, but

145

(11) l - r - Bud Nicholson, Charlie Lewis
Mike Stark (driver) and Hal Moore 1938.

Charlie Lewis and his three LSU roommates purchased this 1929 Model A Ford, touring car (not in mint condition) for thirty-six dollars in 1938. It was their senior year and they wanted to travel. Charlie drove it from Washington, DC to LSU and the four of them used it for duck hunting, fishing and trip to Mexico. The LSU campus police stopped them and threatened to ticket them for not having a windshield wiper. They said, "Why do we need a wiper when we don't have a windshield?" The policeman said, "That's my point." They found a windshield and had it welded on and added a wiper (not sure it worked). It satisfied the police. They sold the car one year later for twenty-five dollars.

all that wealth was stripped away during the Civil War and families never overcame that. Never! Some were fortunate to retain title to their homes, but most of them lost their homes. Of all those ante-bellum homes that are on tour today, very few remained in the name of their original owner. But anyhow, Mississippi's a very nice state. It gets a whole lot of abuse from the press, but it has always been a very compassionate state.

Were you able to earn all your college money doing part-time work or did you have to drop out of school and start again?

I should back up and explain. Back in 1935 I had taken a Civil Service exam for Messenger. You know they give those at most post offices. I passed it. And my first year in college, just before the end of school, I got word that I had a job in Washington as a messenger. It paid ninety dollars a month. It looked like all the money in the world to me at that time so I went up there and worked that summer. When the end of summer came, I had to make a decision: Did I want to stay there in Washington at this high-paying job, be a messenger, compete with other kids and walk the corridor all day or return to Mississippi and get an education? It was a difficult decision to make, but I decided to return to school.

I was very fortunate that the Personnel Director in Washington was captain of the softball team and the Chief of Legal Section was captain of the tennis team. Every department up there had a softball and tennis team. I played shortstop on the softball team and number two on the tennis team, so at the end of summer, I sat down to talk to these two guys and told them the decision I had come upon—that I wanted to return to school.

The Personnel Director said, "All right. Now here's what you can do if you want to come back and get your summer job here next year. Ask for a ninety-day leave, and it will be granted. Before that ninety days is up, you ask for a ninety-day extension, and it will be granted. And before that ninety days is up you ask for another ninety-day extension. That will put you into May. When you get through school you come up here, and you've got your job back."

I didn't want to go back to Washington the summer after my graduation. I had planned to work in Roosevelt's Civilian Conservation Corp (CCC program), but I graduated in 1939 and in 1939 they canceled the CCC program so I hitched a ride on a logging truck to Crosby, Mississippi, and knocked on the receptionist's door. In a matter of ten minutes I had an audience with Mr. Crosby, the president of the company. When I didn't get a job immediately, I hiked it back to Washington.

It was while I was working in Washington that I got this note from the logging superintendent in Crosby offering me a job for sixty dollars a month. That was all a graduate engineer got at the State Highway Department in Louisiana and Mississippi.

It didn't make a lot of economic sense to leave ninety dollars a month to go to sixty dollars a month but I made that decision, severed my ties and allowed nature to take its course.

Washington D.C. is such a glamorous place. After four years you must have found it hard to leave the "movers and shakers" of that exciting city and return to the tranquillity of the Mississippi woods.

No. It really wasn't. All I had seen in Washington was just the routine, day to day, humdrum work. Everything was over-staffed then and probably is ten times as bad now and everyone in government service was looking for some way, some little angle to work, to get a raise or a higher number on their ratings. The bureaucracy was filled with people who didn't have any-thing on the ball and no real desires in life other than to hold onto that job that they had and to get more corporate control. It was a devastating experience. I'm glad I went through it, but I didn't want a part of that anymore.

Did you take the job in Crosby and a lower salary just to escape Washington?

Absolutely not. I wanted to be affiliated with Mr. Crosby. He had bought this old defunct sawmill in Crosby, Mississippi (It was know as Stevenson, Mississippi then) at the height of the Depression. When everyone else was hunkered down, he came over and redid all the railroad tracks, rebuilt the mill, and started it on a two-shift basis and gave jobs and a sense of pride to a lot of people that perhaps would be destitute. Black and white, they were grateful and worked hard to make the opera-tion a success. That mill in Crosby was the biggest ray of hope that was on the horizon in that part of the world. It was very progressive thinking at the time! That's why I made a beeline to Crosby, just as fast as I could, hoping to become affiliated with Mr. Crosby just as soon as I could.

The Crosby family was a very prominent family, a very benevolent family, a gracious family and the old man had gone through this Depression in 1929. He had owned three sawmills at that time, and it was a devastating experience to him, but he tried to hold onto his people. He gave them every opportunity in the world to make it. This is a story unto itself. That noble man made it possible for these people to buy some of these acres for two dollars an acre—and he lent them the money to do that. He lent them the money to build a house. He lent them the money to buy cattle. And he lent them the money to get into the dairy business. He did all this and much more.

What more did he do?

In the center of the town was the huge Crosby commissary and the essential Crosby drugstore. Half the hourly employees' pay was in coupons redeemable in either the commissary, the pharmacy or the picture show. The reason? So the employees and their families need not go without food, medication or entertainment in the event the cash was dissipated—gambling and booze was then, as now, a problem.

He made medical services available and they were considered modern for the time. There was a barber shop, a hair dresser for Negroes and another for whites and a moving picture theater for all. Movies were shown Monday through Saturday and Negroes were relegated to the balcony as was the custom.

How well did that custom actually work?

We didn't have a whole lot of labor disputes, and there were no race relations problems. It's so hard to describe how it was in those days, but there was no bitterness between the blacks and the whites. We never locked our doors. I felt as close to some of them as I did to my own family. We virtually adopted one black family and when Murray wasn't working in the mill, he'd come over to our house and I'd say, "Murray, I don't have anything for you to do today."

And he'd say, "Yeah. that's all right." And he'd take a broom or a rake and go to work. Murray enjoyed just to be there.

You see the blacks were accustomed to this kind of living. The Depression didn't change much as far as they were concerned. They never had any money. From slavery days on up to that time, they were always accustomed to subsistence living.

149

The blacks in Crosby were the exception; they were high rollers. They were very very fortunate! They did have some cash money, but the others who lived out in the country just lived off the soil.

And did the Depression end gradually?

No. Not at all. In 1939, when the Germans invaded Poland, that woke up the world and they realized something bad was happening and everybody decided to do something. Nations that had been lethargic about this like Great Britain and France gave up their thoughts of "peace in our time". Do you remember all this? and Neville Chamberlain? "Appeasement" was the order of the day. But when Poland was invaded, these nations realized appeasement would no longer work. They had to gear up and get ready to fight. It was then that orders began to pour into the United States.

That's when I got out of college. I was fortunate enough to be in on that ascending economic curve. The reason the mill offered me the job was they had just gotten a huge order for prefabricated barracks. Almost overnight, the Depression was kinda history, business was up...and I got a raise.

In 1944 Charlie Lewis married Annie Lee Cannon. They had three children. Before retiring in River Plantation, Conroe, Charlie worked for Crosby Lumber Company, Crosby Chemical Company in DeRidder, Louisiana; Director of Louisiana Forestry Association, Alexandria, Louisiana; Lewis Timber Company in Mississippi (self employed), Georgia Pacific and Louisiana Pacific.

Section III

The Midwest

MARY KRACKLAUER

Violet Kracklauer

Weathering the Depression at a Sioux Mission

My brothers and I were born in the 1940's but we were children of the Depression, not because we experienced food rationing or suffered economic hardships, but because we were raised and inspired by the stories of my mother's cherished experiences "out west on an Indian mission" during the Great Depression.

In 1930, my mother, Violet Wiffler, had recently finished a business college program in Chicago, Illinois and was seeking employment when she read about a secretarial position at an Indian mission in North Dakota. When she requested a letter of recommendation from Fr. Hauck, the parish priest of her small Wisconsin hometown, Arcadia, he attempted to dissuade her from the notion saying, "Too far away from home, too harsh, too lonely. You won't be able to survive." My mother persisted, however, and soon boarded the train for one of the seminal experiences of her lifetime.

Fr. Hauck was certainly correct about one aspect; the conditions were austere and simple, and the comforts few. St. Michael's Mission was founded for the Sioux Indians approximately at the turn of the century and was staffed by the Grey Nuns of French Canada and by Benedictine priests. From the French Canadian influence came the tradition of Catholicism among the northern plains Indians at that time. On the flat, windswept prairie of North Dakota, St. Michael's Mission consisted of a three-story brick dorm and school, the Little Flower Indian School, a small church, and a three-room office building made of logs. During the years that my mother was at the mission from 1931 to 1935, there were approximately sixty-five Indian girls and fifty-five Indian boys in residence, along with ten nuns, four priests, four men and five young women. The priest and nuns were responsible for all aspects of the children's education: academic, social, and religious. The laymen tended the gardens and performed routine maintenance, while my mother and the other young women worked in the kitchen and office. My mother's duties in the office included maintaining records, answering correspondence, and typing the monthly bulletin, "The Northern Lights". For this my mother initially earned five dollars a week, of which she managed to send two dollars home to her family.

With the hopes of obtaining an education and a better life for their children, Indian families from the Fort Totten, Standing Rock, and Fort Peck Indian Reservations brought their six to twelve-year old boys and girls to the mission to board ten months of the year. Some came from tent villages; most came from very poor rural log and sod homes. Despite the warmth of the dorm, the regular meals, and the altruistic care of the priests and nuns, each year some of the young children ran away from the mission back to their homes, many to be returned later to the mission by their parents.

Every year St. Michael's mission was the site of the Sioux Indian Congress, which by the 1930's was primarily a religious gathering. Weeks before the opening of the Congress, the local Indians would prepare for the occasion of the visiting delegates from other regions of North Dakota as well as Montana and Canada. The many tents set up around the mission grounds were reportedly a spectacular sight. In addition to Indian participants with such names as Frank Greyhorn, Henry Ashes, and Henry Grey Bear, many clergy from other missions also attended, and the Indian choirs from the various reservations would take turns singing Gregorian chants during the High Masses celebrated in the tents pitched on the plains way out West.

My mother's photo album is a testament to both the severity and richness of the times. Landscape photos are of terrain that was either flat, dry and dusty, or flat, sparkling and buried deep in snow. In most group photos, the children were dressed alike: sometimes the young boys were all in overalls, sometimes in dark knickers, dark shirts, and white ties. In one photo all of the girls appear to be in communion dresses. How could the nuns sew so many pristine white dresses?

Pageantry and performance were common activities at the

154

mission. In the church basement was a large hall with a stage and two pianos. Mother's album contains photos of Indian children clad in traditional European clothes as well as in oriental clothes with fans. There are pictures of boys' choirs, girls' choirs, and the children playing the piano. Another photo is of young girls, all with the same hair cut and wearing uniforms, playing with dolls in the classroom. One photo shows some typical Depression kids in what looks to be oversized galoshes, black stockings, long skirts, ill-fitting coats with worn fur collars and knit woolen caps - smiling beautifully and proudly from behind their ragged clothing. But always the most fascinating photos in my mother's album were those of the "real Indians" in their real native garb - chiefs with feathers, squaws with braids, children in beads - and sometimes juxtaposed with priests in their flowing cassocks and nuns in their billowing habits.

Two events from those years were repeated many times in my mother's stories to us as children. One was about a car accident. One winter weekend Fr. Damian was driving my mother and a friend into Devil's Lake, North Dakota, the closest town to the mission, when they rounded a bend in the narrow road and suddenly collided with a team of horses driven by a Sioux Indian. My mother flew through the front windshield into a snow bank and was knocked unconscious. The Sioux and one of his horses were killed. When my mother regained consciousness in the hospital, a priest was saying the Last Rites at her side, to which my mother responded, "Well, I'm *not* going to die!" The doctors were not so sure, but fortunately, they were wrong. To the doctors' amazement and despite serious injury to her face and one leg, she did indeed recover. Subsequently the doctors told her, and she in turn often told us, that she had excellent "healing blood", so rich, in fact that the doctors strongly encouraged her to donate it regularly. It was a brush with death that seemed to confirm her love of life, an attitude she sustained into her nineties.

The second experience was the beginning of a profound friendship that my mother maintained her entire lifetime. One of the young women who came to the mission during my mother's second year in North Dakota was Ann Brodeur, a native North Dakotan of French Canadian descent. Mother and Ann readily became very close friends and spent hours sharing the two most common leisure activities at the mission—talking and walking the plains. Through these lengthy conversations, my mother began to suspect that Ann was contemplating joining the order of the Grey Nuns although Ann had not mentioned it directly. I believe, in fact, she had even denied it. My mother's insightfulness was very keen, however, and she told her friend, "Ann, if you ever decide to join the convent and to give up your worldly possessions, please give me your little blue butterfly pin to remember you by." No more was spoken. On the day that my mother left the mission to return to the Midwest, Ann accompanied her to the train station. As my mother departed, Ann handed her an envelope to be opened on the train. In the envelope was the butterfly pin with a note saying, "Now you know my plans. Your friend forever, Ann." And indeed they were friends forever despite the different paths of their lives, one as a missionary nun journeying from North Dakota to the Northwest Territory, north of the Arctic Circle, and the other as a married woman with three children journeying from Wisconsin to Texas, south of the Mason-Dixon Line. These two women of the Depression era remained dear, dear friends all their lives and corresponded for more than seventy years.

My mother's experiences "out west on the Indian mission" significantly affected us as well as her. Certainly she drew great strength from her experiences. She survived the harshness of the environment as well as the Depression, she looked death in the eyes and saw life, and she made an enduring friendship, the kind that many people only dream of. But we, her children, also learned from her experiences at the Indian mission. We learned that she was indeed strong and healing and loyal and that we could depend on her. We learned that she had a sense of adventure and that she was not afraid of risks or the unknown. And most importantly, we learned that these were qualities worth emulating. When life presented its challenges, she would refer to her "Indian days out west during the Depression", and we would know, that like our mother, Violet Wiffler Kracklauer, whatever challenges we had to meet, we could.

Violet Wiffler returned to Chicago, Illinois in 1935, worked for the WPA for several years, and married Aloysius Kracklauer on February 3, 1940. They had three children while living for twenty years in the Chicago area. In 1960 they moved to Conroe, Texas. From Conroe she continued her spirit of adventure by traveling to many foreign countries in Europe, Africa, South America and Asia. Violet Wiffler Kracklauer passed away on March 1, 1995.

(12)Violet Kracklauer far right and the other young women who worked in the kitchen and office

MORNA SMITH

The Depression in a Company Town

Many people remember the Depression years as the worst years of their lives. I do not. They were my growing up years and most of my memories of that time are happy ones.

In 1929, I was in the eighth grade, looking forward to high school in a little town in the Cumberland Mountains of Kentucky. It was founded and named by the Stearns Coal and Lumber Company. It was truly a company town. Everything was built and owned by the company; even the school and one church.

It was customary to give diplomas to the eighth grade graduates at the commencement program for high school graduates. We didn't wear caps and gowns, however. The girls wore white dresses and the boys wore white pants with dark coats.

My mother made a white chiffon voile dress for me. It had a Bertha collar and three flounces for the skirt, all picoted instead of hemmed.

I was fortunate because my father never lost his job. But some of my friends' fathers did, and they had a hard time. Father did take several salary cuts but we never went hungry. With Mother's frugal ways, he managed to keep up the payments on the home they had built in 1922.

Mother made many pretty outfits for four growing girls. She was "a gifted seamstress" and would design, cutting the patterns out of newspapers to fit each of us. One of my favorites was a white coarsely woven cotton that looked like Irish linen when it was starched. It was made out of cow feed sacks. We had a cow most of the time, chickens, and a pig or two. Mother took care of them and raised lots of vegetables in her garden.

We children helped her. We carried water from a spring, brought in coal and wood for the stoves, and ironed our clothes on Saturday. Mother canned and dried vegetables from her garden, as well as wild berries.

We always had a car, from the first Model T. Father needed one, as manager of one of the company's commissaries. He paid a friend to teach me to drive when I was fifteen, a sophomore in high school. He thought it was safer for me to drive us to school because state highway 27 had become a national interstate, with lots more traffic. Mountain roads did not have very wide shoulders for us to walk on.

There was a county school we could have gone to, but it was farther away. The employees of the company voted to pay double taxes for hiring qualified teachers and maintaining a school closer home.

The year 1933 was the year I graduated from high school. It was the year that my older sister, her husband and baby moved back home because he was laid off from his job as clerk in the company's wholesale department. A few months later, he found a job with a mining company in Clenchmore, Tennessee.

I knew it would be too hard on my family to send me to college, so I enrolled in a business school closer home.

The next year I began working temporary jobs for company employees taking vacations.

I began dating my future husband at eighteen, but thought that was too young to marry. Also, he dropped out of school to work in the saw mill. He had to, because there were ten children in his family.

I dated other young men for about a year and a half.

Then, in 1935, a cousin visited us and I hosted a party for her. I invited my future husband. He came and wanted to start dating again. I told him to call me when I returned from a trip I was taking the next day.

He called the day I returned and wanted to take me to a movie. I told him I would meet him at the theater because I was walking with my younger siblings to the movie. Father had to use the car that evening.

When we arrived, he was sitting in the soda fountain adjoining the theater with a very pretty girl I had never met. He introduced her to me and said she was a cousin of the girl working there. I knew her. Her cousin was from Cincinnati.

He went into the theater with me but didn't seem interested in the movie and excused himself to join the pretty girl.

He came back after a short time and asked if it would be all right if he didn't walk home with me.

I've never really determined what happened to me that night. Was it the long walk home under a full autumn moon, seeing him with a pretty girl, comparing him with the other young men I had dated?

I told him it would be fine if he didn't walk home with me, and he needn't call me again. He went out again, came right back and assured me that he wanted very much to walk me home.

Whatever happened to me, when he kissed me goodnight, I knew I would date no one else.

I'm inclined to believe it was the pretty girl. I thought she was prettier than I was and she had a super figure. She was wearing a beautifully fitted hand crocheted purple dress, with pink trim.

From that night on, the most important thing to us was being together. It didn't matter that he had little more than an eighth grade education, a few months of high school and no trade. We were in love and we would make it, together. It didn't matter that my wedding ring cost five dollars and the dress I wore was a blue crepe that I made myself. It didn't matter that we had no money for a honeymoon.

After we were married four months later, in the county court house, we went to eat lunch at my sister Marguerite's house. She had prepared it earlier and went with us to get married.

As soon as we finished lunch, we were going to Clenchmore to bring Marguerite's husband home for the weekend.

Marguerite and our younger sister Dorthie went with us. I drove the family car.

It was December 14, 1935 and the sun was shining, melting a deep snow. However, it had not melted the snow on Clenchmore Mountain. We had to go up seven miles and down eight. We met a snow plow coming down as we started up, and decided not to put the snow chains on the car, as Father had advised us. Almost to the top of the mountain, the car began to slip and slide. The others got out and pushed until we reached a passing lane. Lewis, my new husband, tried to put the chains on but could not fasten them, so he wrapped them between the spokes of the wheels.

We made it up the mountain and about half-way down,

when the chains locked the wheels. We left the car and started walking. Pretty soon we met a car. The driver recognized Lewis; they had played baseball together. He drove us back to the car and cut the chains. We drove on to Clenchmore, arriving just before dark.

We were supposed to be back home before dark. We tried to telephone home, but the lines were down because of the heavy snow. We decided to spend the night. There were no vacant rooms in the boarding house, but there was another bed in my brother-in-law's room, as well as a fireplace. All five of us spent the night in that room.

Lewis and I sat in front of the fireplace and kept the fire going. It didn't matter, we were together.

The next morning we had a good breakfast with the other boarders and started back up the mountain. Sister's husband rode with us to the top of the mountain, where we met Father, in a rented car.

Sister's husband walked back down the mountain, taking short cuts. Marguerite and Dorthie rode back with Father.

As Lewis and I rode back, we crossed a bridge over Buffalo Creek. We started singing "Shuffle Off To Buffalo". It did not matter that we had missed the party, we were together. We stayed together until death did us part, forty-one years and two days later.

The Depression brought many people from other states through our little mountain town. Some rode freight trains, some hitched rides with truckers and some walked. A few pushed wheelbarrows with their belongings in them. All were looking for work, any kind of work.

One Sunday morning an elderly, neat, clean man knocked on our door as we were dressing to go to church. He asked if we had anything left from breakfast. We didn't. Mother had fed the scraps to the dog. Father told him to try the house across the road, at the top of the hill. Mother told Father to watch him to see if the Hickmans fed him. They didn't, so Father went out and called to him. He invited the man in and Mother cooked breakfast for him and served him in the dining room. We children went on to Sunday school and church.

Another Sunday evening as we were leaving for church, a family was passing our driveway and asked if Father owned the

(13) Morna Smith 1932

vacant garage across the road. He wanted his family to have shelter for the night. He was walking to his brother's in a town in Ohio, where he had a job waiting for him. Our parents missed church that evening, too. Mr. Hickman let them sleep in the garage and Mother fed them. Their luggage was in a wheelbarrow.

After I was married, we lived closer to the railroad and I fed hobos occasionally.

Music was as much a part of my growing-up years as was school and going to church, and doing chores: carrying water from a spring and coal and wood for cooking and heating.

Mother sang as she worked and while she rocked the younger children to sleep, Father hummed or whistled. He bought a banjo and taught himself to play when he was in his Thirties. He bought a Victrola and we listened to records of Italian opera tenor Enrico Caruso, Scottish tenor Sir Harry Lauder, as well as Cumberland Mountain musicians.

Later he bought a Majestic radio and we listened to operas on Saturday morning while we helped Mother.

Saturday evenings we invited friends to come and listen to the Grand Ole Opry from Nashville. This led to the formation of an amateur string band. Within a few years, the band began playing for square dances and eventually made records. Some of the records are buried in the archives of The Congressional Records.

Learning to sing at an early age, I sang in the choir, took piano lessons and sang duets with sister Dorthie. I learned to play the mountain music by ear and would play with the string band occasionally.

I taught our three sons the joy and fun of singing. Son number one sang tenor with his high school a cappella choir, son number two sang with a band and son number three played drums with a band.

My husband was blessed with a fine singing voice but rarely found time to practice. He served an apprenticeship in electrical motor repair and electrical construction after we were married. He rewired the damaged war ships during world War II, built an electrical construction business, and decided to build a sawmill. After operating the sawmill a few years, he built automatic saw dust burners.

The great Depression actually taught us to work hard, manage well, share with others and enjoy the gift of life.

Morna Smith, nee 1915 Morna Belle Hall, lived the first twenty-five years of her life in the Cumberland Mountains, Kentucky. Married in 1935, she reared three sons. After being widowed in 1976, she taught music, science and art at St. James School, Conroe, Texas '77-'87, retired. Her hobbies include music, writing, study of foreign languages, etc. Among other newspapers, Morna published free lance articles in the Houston Post and the Conroe Courier.

MILLIE GAUDINO

No Deprivation on an Illinois Farm

For many years I considered myself to be a child of the Depression. Only in recent years when comparing notes with contemporaries have I realized I didn't really experience the "Great Depression". Never did I go to bed hungry, never did I lack a bed in which to sleep, never did I stand in line for food distributions or handouts, and never did I miss school for lack of suitable clothing.

I lived in a large, comfortable but plain farmhouse on three hundred acres of fertile Illinois farmland. The house had a screened-in porch, storm windows and screens, electricity, and a full bath (even in the 1920's). The upstairs bedrooms were unheated in the dead of winter, but with plenty of quilts, a warm flatiron wrapped in flannel, and a sister to cuddle against, I slept comfortably. The house was full, occupied by my parents, my beloved Irish grandfather, my three sisters, a brother and me, and a "hired" man, who worked nearly as many long hard hours as my father. He received board, room, laundry and a very small wage, which wasn't always regular. He was a very good friend to us children.

The country air was fresh and pure (except when a heavy rain brought a stench from the feedlot). At night the stars were bright and thousands of fireflies sent flickering, shimmering light across the open spaces.

Our three meals a day included meat and potatoes, home-baked bread, eggs fresh from the hen house and milk from the dairy. In the growing seasons we enjoyed asparagus and rhubarb, fresh cherry and apple pies, strawberry shortcake with whipped cream, corn on the cob and all sorts of vegetables, plus a variety of fruits from the orchard and nuts from the trees along the creekbed.

We had kittens and puppies, ducklings and goslings and

(14) Liphardt children, Illinois farm, 1920's
Millie Gaudino blonde 2nd from right

sometimes an orphaned baby lamb. We had haystacks and haymows to climb up and slide down, and even a playhouse constructed from an old hog shed, that never lost its peculiar redolence no matter how much it was scrubbed. Nevertheless it was a playhouse. We had family reunions and picnics, church suppers, county fairs and spelling bees, and were allowed to have friends and cousins spend the night.

My father loved reading and we had books, although never enough. Daily we received the local newspaper and the Farmer's Journal, and a weekly local; and no matter how scarce money was, the Saturday Evening Post and Collier's. Our school library was small and inadequate, but the church we attended had a library of donated books. Before I was in my teens I had struggled through Pilgrim's Progress and had a Gold Star Award for reading all the books of the Bible. I read my father's favorites, the Zane Grey novels, until I asked my mother the meaning of a passage. She took the book but didn't answer me, and I could never find the book again.

It was a rich life in so many ways, untouched by the Depression. What we lacked was money. My mother made all of our clothing, and we had new dresses each year for the Easter and Christmas programs at school and church. Packers of livestock feed and flour used patterned cloth for their sacks, and dresses, aprons and dishtowels were made from them. My mother was our barber, using a cereal bowl on our heads to achieve a straight cutting line. We didn't look fashionable but we were as neat and well-dressed as our companions.

My parents worried about money and bank closings. My father struggled hard and used all the money he made to meet mortgage payments. His pride would not let him give up his farm as many neighbors were doing. My mother's butter and egg money bought all of the family necessities—whatever grocery items we could not produce ourselves, cloth, school supplies, and the few luxuries we had, such as Roman Candles and Sparklers on the Fourth of July.

At Christmas we received one toy, candy and oranges in our stockings, but we waited for Christmas morning as impatiently and eagerly as later generations who received abundance. Years later when my sisters and I were deploring the high prices of our children's Christmas toys, my mother said, "The prices are high,

169

but at least you are able to buy them. We couldn't."

Before my ninth birthday my mother explained there was no money for a gift for me. She must have explained well because I decided to give instead of get, and I spent school recesses, fashioning brightly-colored bookmarks from construction paper for my family. It was not a good birthday! The gifts I thought were so great were not appreciated. My father didn't want to be bothered even to select one. I cried when I left the table and my mother scolded me because she thought I was crying because I didn't receive a gift.

When I was ten, I received a five-dollar first place award in our school district essay contest. My mother encouraged thrift by taking me to the bank to open a savings account. I wish I could remember what became of that account. It should have been something very significant to make up for the joy I would have had in spending a dollar or two of it. It did make an impression as today I am often frugal, almost penurious, and have a guilt feeling about spending money, a trait I share with many children of the Depression years.

Jobless men, walking across the country in search of employment knocked at our door almost daily looking for food or work. My mother had them wash outside at a tree-shaded washstand and fed them on the porch stoop. None were sent away hungry. The county maintained a poor farm and whenever we rode past it, we children waved eagerly at the men sitting outside. We didn't give much thought to their life. In 1932, for the first time in his life, my father cast his vote for a Democratic presidential candidate.

Once I rode our blind pony into a barbed-wire fence, causing a deep gash across my leg. I rushed to the house expecting medical attention, as the doctor (in those days house calls were more common than office visits) was there to give my sister the physical exam required for teacher certification. My mother rushed me out of sight as she didn't have the money for a doctor. She treated it and for days it had an odorous discharge. During my first weeks in high school I was embarrassed because my stocking stuck to the bandage.

Still my mother was always doing the best she could, loving each of us and trying to be a good mother. On one of her trips to town to deliver eggs she bought a new tam for me for the start of my high school days. Even though I didn't wear it, its vibrant red velour is still vivid in my mind.

We children worked during those growing-up years. We picked the strawberries and cherries, planted seeds and pulled the weeds, picked the bugs from the potato vines, carried feed to the chickens and gathered and crated the eggs, and helped with the cleaning and cooking. The chores were endless and no excuses were allowed for failing to finish them.

My oldest sister worked for room and board in the city when she went to high school and college. My next sister didn't go to college, but worked as a "hired" girl at another farm for a pittance. My brother and I were the first in our family to attend a rural high school and we could live at home.

The school didn't have a choice of subjects, but I learned more in high school than any of my three children in their city schools. Enrollment was small and every student was invited to participate in plays and the glee club, but no sports were offered for girls.

Country teens had it over city teens, who had to ride buses or walk on dates. We had to go by car and we went to the various small towns in the area, as well as to the city for entertainment. Boys did the paying when we dated. One would borrow a family car, and the others helped by pooling nickels and dimes for a gallon or two of gasoline. They scrimped together enough money for movies and refreshments and entrance to dances on the way home. Occasionally we did some drinking, but drugs were not a part of our life. If we smoked, it was more often a five-cent "roll your own" bag of tobacco rather than twenty-cent Camels. We called them "coffin nails" even before all the health hazards were known.

My dream at graduation was to study journalism. I could have had a scholarship at a teacher's college, but it required a pledge to teach for at least five years, and I knew I wasn't a teacher. I was heartsick when my mother said it was my sister's turn to go to school and I could work for a few years as a "hired" girl and save some money for tuition. Nothing could have seemed more horrible to me than to be a "hired" girl.

I was elated when this sister chose to get married over going on to school. My father was progressive enough to believe in education for girls if they wanted it, and he felt bad that he did not have the money for mine. He did manage to pay for a year at business college. While going to school I worked weekends at Woolworth's for twelve cents an hour.

Jobs were still hard to find when I finished these courses, and I had to work for a while as a tutor at the business school and part-time at Sears for fifteen cents an hour. With this money I bought my own clothes, even a warm green winter coat.

When I finally found a full-time job that paid twelve dollars a week, I moved into an apartment with a friend. It was tiny with a pull-out sofa bed, efficiency kitchen, Fibber McGee closet, a shared bathroom down the hall, and use of our landlord's phone. Living was great; we were at last free and independent, earning our own way. We went to dances at the Y, dated lots of young men and sometimes took an evening class at a nearby college. We saved money for vacations and rode north to Wisconsin on the Greyhound bus. Even with limited funds, we were able to stay in a lodge by a lake. Meals, swimming, boating, biking and horse-back riding were included. We could not have been happier at the finest resort in the country.

When my pay was raised to fifteen dollars a week, we rented a deluxe apartment with a real bedroom and its own phone and bath. I bought dresses for my younger sister, and for myself a good wristwatch and fur coat. I bought these on "time" and didn't miss a payment.

It was the best of times until my friend married and I couldn't afford to keep the apartment alone. It was at this time with war clouds hovering that I was offered a job for twelve hundred dollars a year at the Office of Price Administration in Washington, D.C. With nothing to really hold me in Illinois, I borrowed twenty-five dollars for train fare and moved to D.C. My parents didn't object to the move; I had the feeling that my father was proud of me.

From the first I loved living in D.C., although I shared a room instead of an apartment. The first opera I saw was "Carmen", performed on a showboat while I watched sitting on the bank of the Tidal Basin. I went to movies, live theater, and concerts. Big bands made appearances weekly at war bond rallies, and we danced at various USO's with army, navy and marine personnel. On weekends we made sightseeing trips around the area, the Blue Ridge Mountains, Mount Vernon and once to New York

City. We shopped at Woodward Lothrop's and stretched our funds to dine sometimes at fine restaurants. The Mellon Art Gallery and the National Art Gallery were free and just across the mall from our "temp" office building. At lunchtime we could grab a quick lunch and have at least half an hour to wander through the galleries. It was thrilling to see the originals of the Old Masters' paintings: Rubens, Titian, Rembrandt, Da Vinci, along with Reynolds, Rousseau, Manet, Degas, Cezanne and many others. The museums and the monuments, the cherry blossoms and the Smithsonian were inexpensive sources of delight. A friend poked fun at my roommate and me because we were so enthralled by all the sights, but we were happy to retain our sense of wonder.

My job was fine, although I felt none of us put as much into our work as we should with war coming ever closer. I learned that in government, then as now, one should never suggest that anyone, even one's self, was doing less than a full day's work, or that a department was overstaffed in order for the chiefs to earn a higher salary. The department heads constantly changed as they were so quickly commissioned into the military. I was the only constant in my department and was unofficially in charge without the title or pay, but I loved the work.

Looking back on those Depression years I see a richness and fullness in my life, not a deprivation. The older people and those with families bore the brunt of the poor economy. The only change I would have wished for was more education. Possibly not having television compensated because we learned to use our own resources for our leisure time. The years did leave a deep impression. I retain the habits of saving and knowing how to work, and the pride in being independent and taking care of my responsibilities—my heritage of the Depression years.

Millie Gaudino began thinking of herself as a writer after winning cash prizes in writing contests when she was nine years old—cash in the Depression years was great. During world War II she was on editorial staff of a War Department Training Journal. But she let other things take priority in her life. In recent years she has been a bimonthly columnist for a local newspaper and an editor on a club publication. Her writing preference is journalism. She has been married over fifty years, has three daughters and three grandchildren, two of whom possess writing talent. She has been privileged to have travel experiences, adventures, hiking in the Himalayas, biking in the Netherlands and Austria, cruising on sailing ships in the Greek Isles and the Amazon in Brazil, a home stay in Bali and many more.

KEN MAC DONNELL

First Jobs and Grownup Experiences

Money was tight, and jobs were scarce in Indiana in the Thirties. Most kids were taught the value of hard work and its relationship to money. When we were twelve years old we were given a dime for allowance per week. There were lots of things you could buy for a dime, such as a magazine, a toy, two packs of gum, a doubledip ice cream cone, or two cold drinks. If lucky enough to get one, we could run a paper route for more money, but the competition was tough and the older kids got these jobs.

Another way to make money was to walk the neighborhoods and knock on doors and offer to mow the lawns. You would find some nice ladies whose husbands had good jobs and could afford this luxury. These were ladies who had no kids, seemed always to have bridge parties, and who we thought were very rich. We got paid fifty cents to a dollar per yard, depending on its size.

High school boys worked in the grocery stores, both the chains and the small independents. You could get "working hours" arranged at school and complete all your classes by noon, by presenting the school with a letter from your parent stating you needed to work.

My first full-time job was on a chicken farm. I spent the summer before my first year in high school on a small chicken farm on the outskirts of town. I lived with the owners of the place from Monday through Saturday morning. The work was keeping the place in order, keeping the grounds, cleaning the chicken houses, gathering eggs, and painting the buildings. The owner and his wife both worked, had no children, and knew my parents. The lady of the house knew what teenage boys liked to eat. She kept the new refrigerator full of cold cuts, cheese, and fruit. She bought candy bars by the box. It didn't matter that they paid me about twenty cents an hour. I ate up another twenty from that heavenly refrigerator.

175

(15) left Ken MacDonnell 1935-36 "The Macs".
    In 1933 Ken took music lessons with a WPA
teacher

When Social Security cards were first required ('37-'38?) I got one of the first issued. During school session I got a job with a neighboring grocer. This shop had groceries, hardware, and a post office sub-station. I drove their old '35 Plymouth with the back seat removed to deliver groceries. This job paid twenty-four cents per hour. It helped put my younger brother through his first year in high school. Mother saved the money, half of my pay. I worked from two o'clock to six in the evening and from 7:00 a.m. until 9:00 p.m. Saturdays. I was counter clerk, stockboy, deliveryman, and cleanup boy. I learned about other grownups and life. I had a special permit to drive at fourteen.

Many adult men made from sixteen to thirty dollars per week at blue collar jobs. Work was an accepted fact of life. You had money if you worked. It was a fact of life like eating and sleeping, and breathing. It was part of survival.

We always heard the phrase "save some money for a rainy day". When we lost a job, or had any major expense, we could not borrow money, or get credit. Almost everyone tried to save back a few "bucks" for leaner times. Without credit cards or time payments, it was necessary to "save up" for whatever we wanted to buy.

Teens were allowed to use the family car on special occasions and saved up for gasoline. If we were lucky, someone had a car for Saturday night to go to the movies, ride around town, or get refreshments at the drive-ins where they had "carhops" to wait on us.

We boys tried cigarettes, pipes, and cigars, and we took pride in dressing up in the latest fashions. Botany Five Hundred, Glen Plaid, double-breasted suits were "in" and cost about seventy-five dollars which was a fortune to us, but worth saving up for, even if it took two or three months of curtailing all the unnecessaries and scrimping. Norfolk jackets with the square shoulders in two-tone colors and belted, were the next classy item. White corduroy pants and jackets were worn to high school where all our friends would autograph them.

By the time we were seniors, some of us bought old, used cars. We wanted better cars but the cost was beyond our means and we were realistic. My first car was a '28 Model A Ford Roadster with a rumble seat. It had a convertible canvas top, dark blue body, and green fenders. The floor in the rumble seat had rusted out, so we kept it closed down.

We all tried beer, sloe gin, and Southern Comfort, on the sly. Afraid of being caught, we chewed mouthfuls of SenSen before going home.

We had choices to make at school and at work. We had to be independent of our parents; however, we were expected to conform to their rules and to respect the full authority of our teachers, employers, and law officers. Drunkenness, traffic violations, and other failures to "do right" were rare, and the punishment plus disgrace and further restrictions, were awesome to us. We complied.

Church holidays never failed to bring respect, wonder and awe to us, but we became more worldly and curious about life and began to form our personal religious beliefs. Many of us remained in our family's faith, but mixed marriages were not uncommon and the attitude about religion was changing. It changed more in the war years that followed in the Forties.

Ken MacDonnell is a nationally published poet, a retired business manager and vice president of the Texas Irish Association. He is native born Irish, a U.S. citizen, educated in U.S. and raised in Indiana. He leads a bluegrass and Cajun band, clog dances, is a member of local poets and writers groups and lives on six acres in Montgomery County, Texas.

GRANT PERRY

A Boy's Life on the Prairie

Hamlin Garland, who wrote, among other things, a book about growing up on the prairie entitled *A Son of the Middle Border*, was able to make that kind of life sound romantic and appealing despite the never-ending round of hard work which his boyhood entailed. For me, life since boyhood has been so different that it has grown hard to recall how it actually was on the North Dakota prairie.

I feel as though I missed something because my dad, perhaps because he thought me delicate, or to keep peace with Mom, never put me to work doing chores until I was old enough to request the privilege, and such requests were sporadic—kids don't consistently ask to be put to work.

Dad had a manure spreader and sometimes when we were quite small, my sister Nan and I would ride along on that. It had a moveable floor consisting of a number of slats on a revolving belt which, when the thing was "in gear," moved slowly toward the back, where a more rapidly revolving cylinder would throw the manure off the back end in a controlled fashion. Thus, there being only a single seat for the driver who controlled the team of horses, the young passengers had to keep walking forward as the machine proceeded in order to stay aboard. Through the eyes of childhood that did not necessarily seem to be an unpleasant thing to do. I'm sure we wore overshoes, and wiped our feet when the ride was over.

Once when I was about three a strong wind took the roof off the barn and, in landing a short distance away, it knocked over the privy. That was a significant event in my young life, and I did not hesitate to tell anyone within hearing about it. That included Othel Nelson, an old maid who had a homestead a mile or so away and came by the house to buy eggs. My mother tried to hush me, but I got the message across. The roof of the barn was replaced, but it was never shingled, which meant, after the lumber had dried out a few years, many cracks and leaks, and a very mucky barn unpleasant alike to cows and milkers. In the summertime we could milk outside, but in winter the milking had to be done in the barn in order not to freeze both teats and hands. A "cow shed" was eventually added, with a crudely thatched roof, between the official barn and what Dad called the "oats bin," which had been a part of the house on the Cinto homestead, but it was not any great improvement.

My dad may seem, from the foregoing description, to have been somewhat shiftless, and perhaps he was, but the significant thing was that the folks never had any money. They did a great deal of making-do. They had (for that time) a large mortgage, which they were trying to pay off in annual payments, whenever the harvest was over each year. Often the crop was insufficient and the price of wheat too low to make the mortgage payments. Sometimes they didn't "get their seed back." The living consisted of what they could grow in the garden, butchering annually or semi-annually a hog and/or a steer; sour cream, which was a cash-producing commodity; and butter and eggs, which could be traded at the store for groceries and other necessities. Eventually, about the time I started college, there was a monthly state old-age pension of twenty dollars or so, which was helpful to Grandma. Sometimes she was talked out of it. Once, I'm sorry to say, her pension went to purchase a cheap Sears Roebuck slide trombone, which I played in the college band.

Although North Dakota was a wheat-producing state, the crop was usually mortgaged and could not be depended upon even to pay off the loans against it. Many a merchant who trusted farmers to pay a grocery bill at harvest time was forced out of business when they weren't able to meet the obligation. In Plaza there was Iver Nelson, as honest and decent a man as I ever knew, whose bankrupt general merchandise and grocery store was displaced by a beer tavern after beer became legal in the early Thirties. The Prohibitionists were certainly right about one thing: A certain class of people could find money for beer whether or not they were able to buy groceries.

Another way by which my parents helped eke out a living was driving a school bus. Mountrail Consolidated School was the only school in the township. Most rural North Dakota townships had a one-room school for all eight grades at each corner of the township (townships being six miles square), with the idea that pupils would walk to school or furnish their own transportation. Ours had one two-room school in the center. The two classrooms were in a semi-basement, it having been contemplated that the population might grow and the building would be expanded upward later. (Instead it was eventually reduced to one room, but that is another story.) There being only the one school, four flexible bus routes were provided, so that roughly an equal number of students could be transported in each of four private automobiles, when the weather was good, or by buggy or sleigh when the roads were not passable by car. Those who wished to drive buses would submit sealed bids, which were usually at rock-bottom prices, an important motivation being that the parents who were successful bidders could see that their own children, as well as the others, were promptly and warmly delivered to the schoolhouse. One year my dad drove our bus for forty-eight dollars and fifty cents a month. A couple of times my mother substituted for hospitalized teachers at twenty-five dollars a week. Normally the teachers lived in a small house (the "teacherage") which was provided for them on the school grounds.

Riding the bus was usually a fun part of the school day. Charcoal footwarmers and blankets or robes were provided in cold weather. Sometimes the driver (especially some of the younger ones) would let the boys ride the runners of the sleigh in the wintertime, or even tie their coaster sleds on behind. The sleighs were covered affairs with benches along the sides and a stove in the center. Sandwiches left over from lunch (we carried our own in those days) could be toasted on the top of the stove.

Sometime in the early Thirties my mother had broken her glasses. Rather than pay the cost of a new frame or new glasses, she made do with a pair that had been prescribed for Dad, which he never wore anyway. (He later bought a pair of dime-store magnifiers to read with.) This was by no means an unheard-of expedient. Grandma and Grandpa used the same glasses, interchangeably. Since Grandpa rarely left the place, the glasses were bought by Grandma to fit her own requirements, and in order to read with them Grandpa had to hold the paper within about six inches of his face. Surely New Englanders, for all their reputation for making do, had nothing on them.

For a number of years, during that time, Mom had no lower teeth. During the comparatively prosperous mid-Twenties, when she was about thirty-five, Mom had her uppers pulled, and laid out the necessary thirty-five dollars for an upper plate; but by the time, six or eight years later, when her natural lowers were no longer viable, she felt that the cost of a lower denture ruled it out of the question. Her heroism was hard on her digestion.

So it is not surprising that I was always acutely conscious of my family's shortage of money. Odds and ends of change that I had earned or been given to spend, like Grandma's nickel when we went to town on Saturday night, I nearly always saved. I always thought several times about things I might want to spend money on, and usually concluded that they were not worthwhile, or perhaps that I was not worthy of them. After two or three years I had accumulated about five dollars in this fashion. I had wanted rather badly to build a crystal detector radio set (capable of receiving strong radio signals without battery or electrical amplification and converting them into sounds audible through headphones), but the five dollars or so that the parts and the long antenna system would have cost would be, I decided, too large and selfish an expenditure just to please myself. To this day I often have trouble spending money, at least on myself.

I never had a riding horse or a bicycle. I used to envy the Ike boys and the Onstad twins, near neighbors, who in each case had at least one horse to share between them. What riding I did was done on Kate, a Belgian draft horse and Dad's favorite. She never galloped—Mom called her a pacer—and we had no saddle; her back was too broad for a saddle in any event. I used to have to hang on tight with my legs to keep from slipping off. I never rode farther than to Grandma's place, a mile or so down the road.

Nowadays when children are deprived, it is often because the parents are self-indulgent, addicted to drugs or liquor, have mental problems, or are simply unrealistic. My parents were none of the above: they were just poor farmers trying to work their way out of it without much cooperation from nature.

The pace of life was slow, and nothing much happened. We stopped to smell the roses—wild, of course, the only kind around—whenever we found any. In the falls of dry years, after the grass in the pasture was eaten up, I used to herd the cows around the small sloughs and rockpiles where there was still a little green grass, an all-day job in the hot sun that I didn't too much relish. I had a five-cent New Testament and a five-cent paperback copy of Swedenborg's *Heaven and Its Wonders and Hell* which I used to carry with me and read during the long hours.

The air was fresh and unpolluted. There were still a few coyotes around, and in the evening we could listen to them singing. Incidentally, the singing of the coyotes and the chanting of the local Indians both were often called howling or ki-yi-ing, but I believe the terms I use are more accurate.

For us the hard years of the Thirties were really ushered in August of 1928, when there was a beautiful wheat crop, and just after harvest had begun a terrible hailstorm came along and wiped the whole thing out in a few minutes. That which had already been cut and shocked was partially salvable, but the rest was a total loss—only slightly covered by state hail insurance.

Like all hailstorms, this one was localized. Where it hit, it was devastating, but fields two or three miles away were untouched. Having little or no harvest of his own to care for, Dad went to work on a threshing rig operating north of Plaza for three dollars a day, leaving Mom and us kids to care for things at home, and that was one time I did some cattle herding—and some milking and turning the handle of the cream separator.

One dry year the folks obtained from the county agent a "shelterbelt," consisting of seedling trees of various species, which they dutifully planted according to instructions, but which, with the drought, the hail, the grasshoppers, the army worms, and the jackrabbits, all eventually died, and in three or four years, of the twelve hundred or so trees originally planted, not one remained alive. Farm life in those days was indeed discouraging.

Drought, hail, grasshoppers, army worms, jackrabbits— the plagues followed one another almost in sequence, like the plagues of ancient Egypt. There were minor ones, too, like distemper in dogs, for which there was no vaccine; and even if the rural areas had been served by veterinarians—and there were some self-styled ones—cats and dogs were expendable.

Grasshoppers in reasonable numbers are normally present on the prairie and lay their eggs in the ground, to hatch the following spring. Usually the winters are severe enough that the majority of the eggs do not hatch; but given a mild winter and dry spring, watch out! Come July with its hot weather, one day you can look up toward the sun and see countless hordes of them. When they land, they eat everything—every bit of growing plant life in their paths. One can hear them chomping away as they proceed in phalanxes along the ground. When they come to a building they march up the sides of it and, if they're hungry enough, they devour some of the wood. The same is true for fence posts and telephone poles. The county agents distributed without charge poison consisting of arsenic mixed with bran which the farmers put out along the edges of the fields. It may have slowed the grasshoppers down somewhat, but its main effect was to kill birds, pheasants, and other wildlife, sometimes including flocks of turkeys, which tend to range unless confined in pens.

Army worms also devoured everything in their paths, but they would clog roads and ditches; you had to be careful driving over them. The chickens would eat them and they would turn the egg yolks a deep red. They seemed to find their way inside the houses more readily. They came on suddenly—you could look up the road and see them in phalanxes slowly advancing toward you—and just as suddenly disappeared.

We had plagues, but we had no Moses, and we had no Children of Israel to let go. There were theories about the causes. One imaginative explanation for the droughts was to the effect that we had upset the weather patterns by polluting the atmosphere with radio waves. The Jehovah's Witnesses, who grew during that period, maintained that Armageddon was just around the corner and that it was all spelled out in the Bible. The air was thick with radio waves carrying the messages of the likes of Father Coughlin, Reverand Gerald L. K. Smith, Huey Long, Westbrook Pegler, William Dudley Pelley, and assorted would-be political demagogues who flourished in hard times, especially in a state like North Dakota with its two state parties, the Nonpartisan League and the Independent Voters Association.

If boyhood ends with the first date, that didn't happen for me until I was in college. It wasn't that I wasn't attracted to girls, but there was no money, no access to a car, and most of all, no encouragement. And I suppose I tended to be rather negative even then. I went stag to the junior prom. When I was a high

(16) Grant Perry

school senior, I was on a religious kick and stayed away from the prom altogether.

Boyhood really does not end all at once. When the time came for me to start high school, the folks rented a small, two-room house in town for five dollars a month. Most of the first year we did without electricity—there would have been a five dollar connection charge and probably a dollar or two a month bill. Mom and sister Nan slept in one room and I in the other, and we spent the weekends out on the farm, where Dad stayed all the time and took care of the livestock. He spent a good part of that first winter practicing penmanship, preparing to write on a civil service examination for auxiliary rural carrier, because he had heard that, other things being equal, penmanship counted. The examination was for an annual job three months of the year, in the wintertime when it was necessary to drive horses to get the mail through, and therefore the regular carrier could not cover a sixty-mile route.

As I recall there were more than thirty applicants who wrote on the examination, and Dad was at the top of the list. Dad, who until that time had always voted Republican, like almost everyone else in the community, became a Democrat and persuaded the local Democratic committeeman to recommend his appointment.

When Dad got his three-month appointment, we moved into town "for good" (as people used to say when they meant "permanently"). That was, practically speaking, the end of this boy's life on the prairie.

Grant Perry is a native of North Dakota. He was born on what the maps still show as an Indian reservation on April 1, 1919. Aside from school, he had no close friends outside his immediate family. He graduated high school in 1935 and college in 1939, taught school a couple of years and entered the army in 1942. In due course, he got out, married, became a court reporter and later a reporter of debates in the U.S. Senate. Meanwhile, he raised a family, was widowed after thirty-seven years of marriage in 1983, married again in 1985, moved to the Woodlands in 1986. Since retirement in 1979, he has written mostly poetry. His book, *Musings and Forebodings* was published in 1993.

WANDA K. MAC DONNELL

Life in a Pole House in Owen County, Indiana

My family lived on Shaw Street in Plainfield, Indiana, where I was born, until my father could not earn enough money to provide for us. This was from 1923 until 1932. He sold apples on a street corner in Indianapolis for a while and operated a fruit and vegetable stand with items he bought daily at the Farmers' Market. This was seasonal work and could not be done on a year-round basis, due to severe winter weather in Indiana.

After the family could no longer afford the necessities of life, such as food and shelter, we returned to the farm in Owen County, where all of our relatives lived.

My grandparents deeded four acres of land to my parents upon which they built a pole house. The poles were the trees that were cleared from the four acres. Thick mud was used to caulk the air spaces between the poles and when dry, formed a secure insulation that protected us from the cold of winter.

We had a wood burning, pot-bellied stove in the front room and a small kerosene, two-burner stove for cooking in the kitchen. There were no partitions, but we knew what the areas were called and used for because of the placement of furniture. We were never too warm, but thankfully we were never too cold.

When spring arrived, we were all freed of our heavy, bulky undersuits, or long Johns, as they were called by some. We looked five pounds thinner, although the undersuits could not have weighed more than one pound, if even that much.

We did not have TV, radio, telephones, or even a newspaper. In fact, I do not remember reading, except in textbooks, until I was fourteen years old and received as a gift, a wonderful book called *A Girl of the Limberlost* by Gene Stratton Porter.

Consequently, we children invented our own games and

sources of recreation. One of our favorites was digging a place to play in the sassafras grove, which was about thirty feet away from the house. Using tablespoons from our mother's kitchen, we dug a hole about a foot deep and three feet in diameter. We carried buckets of water from the pump and emptied them into the hole. We sat on the edge and soaked our feet in the mud that we created. We also made wonderful mud pies from that mud and decorated the tops with fancy designs.

Someone gave us a black and white male kitten. We dearly loved that kitten and named him Tommy, knowing that we would shorten the name to Tom when he grew into an adult cat. We never let Tommy touch the ground when we were outside and carried him with us everywhere we went to play. He was well-loved and was treated like a member of the family until we prepared to move away.

My father learned of a company in Muncie, Indiana that was hiring men for warehouse work. He went there and was hired. Mother and we four children prepared to move and were very sad when we had to leave Tom behind. We were assured that Tom would not go hungry, and would go to a neighboring farm for food. We stayed in Muncie for a year or two and we returned to the pole house for a visit.

Anxiously, we explored the four acres and were pleasantly surprised to discover a huge black and white cat watching us from a distance. Although he was extremely large and seemed to have long thick hair, we knew he was our Tom. We called and called to him, but he would not come to us. Every time we got within a few feet of him, he would turn and run away. We wanted to renew our loving relationship with him, but he was afraid and stayed far enough to prevent us from catching him. We knew he was not going hungry, but we were deeply hurt that he would not trust us enough to let us touch and hold him.

One of the sternest lessons we learned was that of being practical, instead of making emotional decisions in times when the basic needs of humans were difficult to meet.

Wanda was born in Indiana and spent the first twenty years of her life there. After she married her husband, Ken, they moved to Florida and in 1955 moved to Texas where they stayed. She studied elementary education and holds a BS and MS from the University of Houston. She is now a retired school teacher. After rearing three sons, she has extra time, which she spends writing and playing violin. Wanda belongs to and is a past president of the Scribblers Club in Conroe, Texas. She is also a past president of River Plantation Lions Club in Conroe. She is a violinist in Symphony North of Houston and also plays fiddle in the Shadetree Bluegrass Band with her husband who plays five-string banjo. She enjoys retirement, but likes to stay busy.

(17)Wanda MacDonnell back row right with sisters and brother, Vera, Mona, Ovid - 1939

189

JEAN NASH WILLCOX

Looking Back

In 1929 the stock market crash introduced the Great Depression, and I graduated from high school in Saginaw, Michigan. There were no jobs available. With my parents' cooperation I was able to stay in high school for a post-graduate year of business courses.

After that, life was a Spartan menu of temporary jobs. It took me eight years to get through two years at Central State Teacher's College and two years at the University of Michigan. I was lucky to have the typing and shorthand, which helped me prepare my own assignments—and sometimes provided me with small perks from typing papers for my classmates.

My younger brother dipped into his earnings from building state highways to pay my tuition bills. At the same time he kept his sights on Law School (a family tradition). My mother received small commissions from rewriting failed insurance policies for the Lady Maccabees, a fraternal organization trying to keep its membership together. My father's law practice jogged along with the help of fees paid sometimes with paint jobs from unemployed clients, or a bushel of potatoes or a live turkey from those who lived out in the county. It was a time of sharing. He shared advice with my two older brothers, who were working their way through the university to pass their law exams.

There was one memorable summer that my mother and I spent at the Century of Progress, the Chicago world's fair, in 1933. She was in charge of the Michigan Exhibit, which was staffed by representatives of various parts of our state. My mother kept me under her wing. Along with a small group of young women, I had a job, selling fruit juice (tomato, apple cherry—all Michigan products). Since our low wages would not support the juice sellers away from home, they were recruited from the Chicago area. However, they brought fun to the work by

191

inventing stories for the customers about their "hometowns" in Michigan.

At the end of the summer I returned home and became the "Society Editor" of the *Detroit Labor News*. Andy, the editor, and I shared a double desk in the old Detroit Labor Temple of the AFL. Our office looked out on a back alley, with the Window Cleaners Union handy next door. They had lively card games between part-time jobs.

After that experience I found other occupations. I worked a year or so on the trade journal of the FTD (Florists' Telegraph Delivery) where I wrote captions for photographs of bridal bouquets and table centerpieces. Later I answered the siren call of New York, and moved East. My first job there was at Harper's publishing house, where I served two bosses—a man and a woman (a woman's libber before the title was invented). She quickly discovered my Achilles Heel, which was my lack of experience—I didn't know how to bluff. So she arranged to have me "let go."

Gradually I approached the environs of the writing profession. I spent six months as a ghost writer (and I do mean "ghost"), telling the first-person story of a man's life. He was born with tiny embryonic legs that were completely unadaptable.

After he reached manhood, walking on clumsy boots attached just below his hips, this lad met a highly skilled orthopedist. There were grilling months of surgery and countless procedures and adjustments. Finally he emerged with a pair of artificial legs (supported by size 8 1/2 willow feet), almost twice his former height, with a new wardrobe and personality to match. He had faced his trial with bravery and imagination.

He started working in rehabilitation. Gradually he was surrounded by young disabled men and women, who worked in his office in a large New York hospital that served many charity patients.

My problem was to assist him in telling his story to the reader without sounding braggadocial. It was a challenge.

"I know what a remarkable person you are," I would say, "but we must convey this idea without telling the reader directly."

His literary agent was one of the best in the city. She insisted that, since I had no regular income, my percentage of publishers' payments against royalties must come first.

I did not request a byline, or an "as told to" arrangement. It was unthinkable in those days. I was thrilled to have the job, and it worked out very well.

When the book was finished, the author invited me to accompany him to the *Reader's Digest* at Pleasantville, for a conference with top editors about the possibility of his story appearing in the magazine. Some editorial bigwigs were there, including a husband-and-wife team. I believe she was going to write the article and he was acting as her agent.

I never understood why I was included in the group, except that Hank introduced me as a member of the staff of his literary agency. Whereupon I disappeared into a small corner.

Ten years later, in 1963, I was invited to the *Digest* for a job interview. I can't recall who initiated this, if I ever knew. It may have been an agent or an editor, or someone I had met in a work situation. I remember joking about it to a friend who wrote editorials for a left-wing magazine. I didn't want to go.

He surprised me by insisting I have the interview, so I reluctantly agreed.

After four or five meetings with personnel and editorial staffers in ascending order, I was offered a job as copy editor of Condensed Books. And I accepted. What a change in my status from that first visit.

I stayed for sixteen years and retired on my birthday. However, I must say that my progress from the detailed factual editing into the areas of book selection, dealing with story, plot and character, taking authors to lunch, could not have succeeded without a company-wide support group.

A sturdy band of women employees braver than I started a class action suit, demanding that they be subject to the same job requirements and pay as the male employees. There was tension and hush-hush. None of us chatted with the men, who worked across the hall, while the suit was in preparation. When the women's attorney contacted me, and asked if I would tell my story to the judge, I agreed to do so, but I was very uneasy.

The morning of my pre-trial testimony I was almost dysfunctional. I had carelessly let a window at home slam down on my thumb. An hour later when my attorney and I sat opposite the six-foot-two interrogator representing the company, I kept my bandaged ice-packed hand under the table. As the other attorney talked, my ally kept passing me notes that read "shorter answers...too much detail..." which kept me going.

At the very last minute the suit was settled out of court. The morning we received the news, my friend Tony, a fellow editor, came out of his office to shake hands. "Now we can speak to each other again," he said. "How about lunch?"

I retired on my birthday in 1979. Despite Management's offer—to keep me on the staff, in accordance with my new legal rights—I declined.

Jean Nash Willcox was born in Saginaw County Michigan January 1, 1914. After the Depression in the late Thirties she graduated from the University of Michigan with a Liberal Arts Degree. Widowed early in World War II as a bride of a few months when her husband was killed overseas, she enlisted in the U.S. Navy serving as a Wave. Following the war she became a free lance writer in New York City until a long period of employment at the *Reader's Digest* as Editor in Chief of the *Condensed Books* where she served until her retirement to Boulder, Colorado where she now resides.

(18) Jean Willcox 2nd from right

(19) Jean Willcox 2nd from left

195

BLANCHE B. PAPACEK

Hardly a Ripple in My Life

Just now, seventy years later, I begin to realize the challenges which faced my parents during the Depression in Illinois.

My father was a men's clothing and shoe salesman in a department store. He worked six days a week plus Thursday and Saturday evenings to 9:30 p.m. There was no forty hour work week then. My father worked hard at his job and yet I never heard him complain about his work or its disadvantages. I do not remember his ever taking a day off from work or having much vacation time. He would discuss things with my mother about an employer's attitude or a customer's but never about the sameness of the job or the long hours.

Incidentally, at this time, women did not go out of the home to earn money inasmuch as the job of being a "bread-winner" was deemed a man's job, while a woman's job was the care of home and children. It would have been demeaning to my father if my mother would have gone to work to earn money, and I am glad my mother's consideration of my father's feelings gave him the confidence and the chance to have the freedom and the opportunity to fend and provide for his family.

This was put to the test when the Depression became most severe and my father lost his job. Unemployment insurance was unknown at that time, and money in order to live was needed. This is what gets my utmost admiration as my father did not get depressed and sit at home. He applied for and became a Watkins salesman going door to door in surrounding neighborhoods selling the Watkins products: cocoa, vanilla, baking powder, and various other items which I now do not remember. He also later became a Fuller Brush man. He met his challenge of no work in such a way that, I, as a child, didn't really realize that a Depression was going on. It is only now that I'm realizing what it meant to my parents.

The economy finally got better and my father resumed his original selling type of job, but to me the Depression was hardly a ripple in my life. I'm very grateful for this. I know that our family was not unique - all over America this same spirit of not giving up when things get tough was and, even now, is going on. I'm very grateful for all this. The following poem is, I believe, in keeping with the above:

IN "MY DAY"

"Back then," you ask how was it?
Listen child, and I will tell it.
A man was a man, not a boy;
A woman was a woman, not a toy.
A man knew his home was a haven;
A woman's job was to make it a heaven.
A child felt the warmth, comfort and unity,
Without upheaval or instability.
I'm not contrasting this with things today,
Just telling how it was in "my day."

After the Depression Blanche Papacek married and had three children. After twenty years the family left Illinois and settled in California. Thirty years later they went to Texas and lived there almost five years. They now live in the Valley of the Sun in Arizona. She says she loves each of these states in this beautiful and wonderful land of ours.

Section IV

The Northeast

ANNETTE SCHWARTZ

Family Support During the Depression

Married in 1922, my parents enjoyed a middle-class lifestyle until the crash of 1929 when my father lost his job as a clothing salesman. They had three children in the first six years of their marriage. A hyperactive child, the eldest of three, I climbed trees with the boys, played baseball in the streets and swam in a city pool during summers in Buffalo, New York. Life was pleasant before the Depression.

My mother Pearl, was one of eight girls. My father, Nathan, had five sisters and brothers. I had many cousins. I wore hand-me-downs from a cousin whose father ran a tavern, a business that did not suffer during the Depression. An old photo of myself and two brothers, taken in the 1930's, wearing inexpensive clothing in a barren backyard without grass, trees or flowers, reveals how poor we became. Many of my cousins had as little as I did, but my parents compared me to a cousin whose father owned a profitable dry goods store. Dressed in dainty dresses, she sat quietly, had excellent grades and never got down on her hands and knees to play marbles. With excellent hand-eye coordination, I had a large collection of steelies and glassies but this was not the kind of success my parents were looking for.

My aunt Celia and Uncle Morris also lived in Buffalo. They owned a grocery store near an exclusive residential neighborhood, invested in the stock market and bought a two-family house in that area though they lived behind their grocery store. In 1929 they lost most of their investment in the stock market and could not rent the expensive house they owned. My father was no longer able to pay rent where we were living so they let us move into the lower half of the house and rented the upper half to the man who delivered groceries for them and earned very little also.

My father found a job cleaning city streets one day a week

(20) 1930 The Sterman family
Annette Schwartz far right

to earn some money. He also sold clothing on consignment in an open air market where he often took food from the farmers in payment, then shared it with people who had less than we did. Living in an area where neighborhood children came from families who could afford all the things I wanted for myself, only made me feel more deprived than ever. Pretty party dresses with ruffles, lace and ribbons, swimming, dancing and horseback lessons were but a dream for me. When I complained, my father took me to a dilapidated residential area on the waterfront and pointed out the children playing outside shacks with broken windows.

Summer camp was out of the question. My only vacation was a visit to my Aunt Chia who lived in Toronto, Ontario, in Canada, a two-hour drive from Buffalo. She had a grocery store near the downtown commercial area where the rent was very low. Her customers were all on welfare. Aunt Chia lived behind the store. She cooked, cleaned, did bookkeeping and many other chores between the few times she was busy with customers. She had to feed, dress, move her husband from chair to chair, as his health deteriorated from Parkinson's disease. A generous, affectionate and patient person, she never complained when I used an orange crate as a counter, outdoors, and sold candy taken from her store to people passing by. I ate as much as I sold. She also let me choose a different flavor carbonated drink each day, a treat I never had at home.

My Aunt Hinda, a widow with two daughters a few years older than I, let me pick out any dress I wanted from her small shop each time I came to visit. My Aunt Rose, also a widow with one daughter, had a tiny dry goods store in a suburb of Toronto near my Aunt Hinda. They both lived behind their stores in a very poor neighborhood, barely made enough profit to live on, but shared what they had. To entertain me, my cousins took me to Sunnyside, an amusement park near the beach. I had fun but it didn't seem like much of a vacation compared to the expensive camps children from my neighborhood attended. Looking back, I realize how fortunate I was to be part of such a loving and compassionate family.

My relatives in Buffalo were good to me too. My Aunt Celia's store was half-way between our home and the local theater where my two brothers and I went every Saturday afternoon. On our way home, we stopped at their store and Aunt Celia served us supper using food that did not sell well and fruit that was almost over-ripe. It was then that I learned the secret of enjoying flavorful fruit was eating it just before it began to spoil. Before we left she also allowed us to choose a cookie from a tin container with a glass lid, displayed in her store. We chose chocolate-covered marshmallow cookies each time.

My parents could not afford movies after my father lost his job. However, one day my mother suggested they go to a Shirley Temple movie because she thought he needed to take his mind off his worries. Depressed by the responsibility of providing for a wife and three children without a steady income, he exploded, "Spend ten cents for a movie!" They went. He usually took my mother's advice.

My father found a job as a salesman in a men's clothing store in Jamestown, New York, but my mother refused to move until she was sure it was permanent, so he rented a room and commuted. The job lasted six months.

Several of my aunts and uncles agreed to use some of their meager savings to help Nathan start his own business. My father chose a store in a run-down neighborhood because he did not want to spend too much on rent and stocked it with men's clothing in all sizes, arranged carefully and neatly. The first day the store was open he sold a lot of merchandise. My mother brought him lunch and was pleased to see how well everything was going.

When my father did not return home at dinner time, she went to the store to see what the problem was and found him unconscious on the floor, bleeding. He was taken to a hospital and treated for concussion, cuts and bruises. He said two men had come in just before closing time. While one of them held his attention by pretending to be interested in buying a suit, the other hit him over the head with a pipe. They took all his money and some merchandise.

My parents decided it was too dangerous to stay in that neighborhood and took a loss when they closed the store. Doctor and hospital bills accumulated. They had no insurance.

An old friend told my father that one of the dairies was offering a horse and wagon for home deliveries to anyone who wanted to start a new route. A super salesman, my father started delivering milk and dairy products in a suburb and built up a lucrative route, winning incentive points to bring home many items including a pressure cooker, bathroom hamper, even a refrigerator. But my parents denied themselves many things they wanted to save enough money to pay their debts.

As soon as my father had a steady income, we moved from the lovely but expensive neighborhood where we had been living to a middle-class community. We made new friends and were happy there. However, in 1935, when my mother accidentally became pregnant at the advanced age of thirty-six, she announced that we needed a bigger house. It was difficult to find anyone who would rent to a family with four children. Desperate, they turned to the family again for a down payment and bought a two-family house in the same neighborhood, using income from the other half to help pay the mortgage. Gradually, everything did improve. In addition to his job at the dairy, my father found a second job selling men's clothing, evenings and weekends, to earn enough money to pay the family members who had lent us money to buy our home. I lived in that house until my marriage.

Annette Schwartz was born August 21, 1923. She finished three years of college at Buffalo State Teachers College. She has four children and eight grandchildren. She has qualified for four National Senior Olympics in swimming and bowling, won prizes in the Poetry Society of Texas, and in other poetry contests. She says every day is a celebration of life filled with happiness.

WILLIAM H. LAUFER

Fragments of a Life

April 2, 1934: Natal Day. My mother, Kate Davis Krudop from Stone Mountain, Georgia, who is in the final phase of a terminal illness, delivers me, William Thomas Krudop, into the world in Newark, New Jersey, my father's home. Her husband, my father, William Russell Krudop, is unemployed. She spends the last four months of her life with me in Washington, D.C., where her brother, James C. Davis, is a Congressman, and where my father looks for work. After she dies when I am four months old, the larger family skein of Davis and Krudop pulls together and I am farmed out to a farm—literally—in Alabama to gain health and weight. I stay there one year. We are an Anglo-German family, my brother Charles, seven; sister Catherine, five; and me.

1934-1936: My brother and sister live with various members of the Krudop family, six sisters and one brother: Claire, Alice, Anne, Mary, Roberta, Grace, and my father Russell. Claire is married to William Angelman, who owns a yacht. She takes to her old bed in our grandmother's big house in Newark after her husband loses his fortune and his yacht. Roberta is married to a New Jersey lawyer. Alice marries Archibald Talbot, an Englishman from Bermuda who is Exchequer of the Treasury and who later receives the OBE from the Crown. Mary is married to Hervey B. Marsh from Pittsburgh, who owns the Hervey B. Marsh Insurance Company, which goes into bankruptcy. He dies during this period. Anne marries a Mississippi businessman Walter Gough, and when his paper box business fails, they move into the Krudop home. Grace, who would eventually become our new mother, marries Edward B. Laufer, a mechanical engineer and the son of a Pennsylvania German Presbyterian minister and hymn-composer (Calvin Weiss Laufer). In 1937 Edward

207

quits his job as an engineer with Public Service Utilities of New Jersey and goes to work in Wall Street as a Securities Analyst. (He dies in 1987, a multi-millionaire.)

We three Krudop children are adopted by Edward and Grace Laufer in 1938. I am renamed William Hervey Laufer, the "Thomas" which my mother chose being dropped in favor of the name of Aunt Mary's husband Hervey Marsh. We have lived briefly in Montclair, then with Ed and Grace (as we always call them) in West Orange. In 1938 we move to the three-story house on Tillou Road in South Orange, our permanent home.

1937-1938: During these years, the several husbands of the Krudop sisters meet with financial misfortune. William Angelman, Walter Gough, and my natural father, William Russell Krudop, move back into the family manse at 547 Broadway in Newark, a large Victorian house with only one bathroom. Hervey Marsh dies of a ruptured spleen. Roberta's husband, Arthur Harris, a lawyer, dies of a massive heart attack (and Roberta remarries a Bermudian in the Forties). When Claire dies, her widower William Angelman marries Mary Marsh, his widowed sister-in-law. My staid step-father would tease Mary about sex in her sixties. Anne does not remarry. My father, called Russ, eventually becomes a traveling ribbon salesman and marries a woman named Donny from Nebraska. He would later have died in poverty but for the help of my sister.

In 1939, this enormous family is all together on the Nantucket-Woods Hole ferry headed for Cape Cod. My uncle William Angelman spots a submarine on the surface and says, "I'm glad it's one of ours."

In the neighborhood where I live, I have to stand my ground against prejudice: first, because it is suspected by some that Laufer is a Jewish name (We are Anglo-German Episcopalians.) and then, as war with Germany looms, because we are German.

We are always more English than German. In the early Forties the New Jersey police arrest our maid, Ilsa, and our South Orange neighbor Mr. Mennen of Mennen After-Shave products because they are German. (This signals the end of the Depression. War is upon us, and war is good for business.) My first memory of fire comes in the Forties when we watch ships burn off the Jersey coast.

The Depression forces change upon our culture at the

208

deepest levels. It is not only economic displacement but societal displacement as well. The family myth holds that my brother, sister and I grow up together as a family. We do not. We are displaced by the general confusion of the times.

We are never a family. We live under the same roof for various periods of time, but we never do so as brother, sister, and brother. Catherine is sent off to boarding school and Charles lives his own protected life immersed in piano. By my tenth year I am sent off weekly, by myself, to Newark by train to take violin lessons. One constant is Florence, a black woman who replaces Ilsa on the third floor of our house (and who is still there, in charge, after Ed dies in 1987—Grace having died in 1967).

Our step-mother Grace always insists, from some strange standard of her own, that we are poor. We children have no standard of comparison for this, and we believe we are, when in fact we are not. No one who lives on the side of South Mountain in South Orange is poor. Clarence S. A. Williams, who lives across the street, has made his fortune as the Chief of Staff for Thomas A. Edison. Our neighbor to the north is Frank McCann, a contractor who later builds the United Nations Building in New York, and the maiden name of our neighbor to the south is Aronson, of the Ronson Lighter fortune. I have already mentioned Mr. Mennen. Charles' nearby sometime girlfriend is Barbara Pabst, of Pabst Blue-Ribbon beer.

Lessons from the Depression can be drawn from the disciplines of economics as well as from cultural anthropology. A simpler rationale, however, may apply: the rain falls, and it falls with equal vigor on the just and the unjust.

Of the Depression I think this: my experience of it reflects the values of the Northeast at that time: we had lost our ties to nature; we were materialistic and progress/prosperity driven; family values had been de-emphasized; our economic system had failed along with many of our institutions. If my reflections appear fragmented, it is because that was the nature of life in that region then. It is my belief that alienation, our great sickness of the present time, entered our lives then because we no longer had defenses against it.

I also think that Paradise, in a biblical sense, is here and now, in Texas, for example, and that the Fall from Paradise occurred *there*, in the Northeast, during the years that led us to the Depression.

Since the Depression, William H. Laufer has obtained an education from Trinity College, The New School, SUNY, Albany, and the Glassell School. He has completed over twenty years service in the U.S. Navy, rising through the ranks from Seaman to Lieutenant Commander. He is a combat veteran of the Vietnam War, the Bay of Pigs Invasion, and the Korean War (and he says every brushfire, nearly, in between). For three years he edited a trade magazine for the Maritime industry in New York, and served as operations manager for a steamship company there. His fiction, non-fiction and poetry has appeared in journals in the U.S. since 1953, and he have completed three hand-made and hand-printed artist's books as author and artist. Since the 1970's he has worked as an artist-printmaker, and his work has been shown throughout the U.S., Europe and Asia. He says, happily, his best friend and wife is Guida Jackson, Ph.D. Happily, also, he is a naturalized Texan.

MARVIN J. ENGEL

Street Games in the Thirties

I grew up playing on the streets in the south end of Albany, New York. The electric street car rumbled past my bedroom in the flat upstairs over my father's bakery shop. Through the bedroom window, I looked out on a Belgium block paved street with trolley tracks running down the center and power wires strung overhead at about eye level to my second story view. The clamor of iron wheels on iron rails could be distracting to an unconditioned outsider, but it was just part of the background like a lot of other street sounds. The street was narrow for a main street of commerce. Parking was allowed on only one side, which left barely enough width for two vehicles to pass going in opposite directions.

My neighborhood friends and I—we were not thought of as a gang in those days—played street games. There wasn't a playground or a park nearby.

Cross streets were more residential with less traffic and better suited to our play since the frequency of interruption was much reduced. However, play time on these streets was for the most part limited to daylight hours. The exceptions were usually those games requiring stealth and concealment. Street lamps were fewer and dimmer and there were hardly any storefronts to light our playing field.

The main street where the trolley ran was where the action was. Wall to wall storefronts, bright street lights and the competitive challenge of moving traffic and shoppers made an exciting venue for our after dark activities.

Besides Touch Football, played with a stuffed paper grocery bag, and Fifty-more, a form of hide and seek, we (mostly the boys) played such ubiquitous games as Johnny-ride-the-pony, Chestnuts, and the lesser known Five Fingers and Triggy.

Girls played in the streets or on the sidewalks too. Among

the more popular games were Hopscotch, Jump Rope, Jacks and a kind of Simon Says called May I. On occasion, one or perhaps two of us boys would be coerced into playing in one of these games with the girls. It was surprising how inept we were, whether from being unpracticed or from not wanting to be sought after more frequently, especially when in sight of our peer group.

I will describe in some detail the latter four of the boy's games as I believe these are virtually unknown by today's youngsters and very likely by their parents as well.

The game which we called Johnny-ride-the-pony has been referred to by more than a hundred other names depending on where it was played. Two sides are chosen. Ideally, since strength and tenacity are prerequisites, both larger and smaller boys would be distributed evenly. Each of the players on one side bends over in a leap frog position, shoulder to rump, firmly grasping the one in front with the forwardmost player standing erect facing the others, back braced against a wall or utility pole and acting as a linchpin holding his teammates from pitching forward. The opposing team of players, one at a time, leap as far forward as they can over and onto the backs of the first side. They continue in succession until either the bent-over side collapses under their weight and/or impact, at which point they declare themselves winners. However, if the leaping players cannot all attain a seated position on the backs of the bent-over side, or if they do but not for an agreed time interval after the last player has leapt on, then the bent-over players are the victors. After completion of a game, the teams change places and resume play.

The residential streets just a block or two off the main street were lined with mature shade trees among which were horse chestnut trees. In season, these huge trees dropped or were encouraged to drop their pods so that we could gather and extract the chestnuts within. Thus, the game of Chestnuts, adopted from the English game of Conkers became popular in our community.

The game of Chestnuts is a gladiator-like contest employing a horse chestnut suspended on a cord or shoe lace, the free end of which is wrapped around the hand of each of two competing players. The object is to dislodge, fracture or crack your opponent's chestnut by swinging yours to strike his held stationary, and vice versa in turn. Innovative techniques and finite

212

rules pertaining to selection, pre-conditioning and assembling of the chestnuts were an intricate part of each encounter, which often took on the status of a tournament among contestants engaging in one on one combat.

We also played very competitively an unconventional marbles game using glass marbles referred to as "alleys", and sometimes ball-bearing balls known as "steelies". The game, called Five Fingers, was played in the grime of street gutters, adjacent cracked walkways and patches of surrounding muddy turf which provided the necessary adherence for the player's marbles.

Each player, two or more, positions his single marble within the agreed boundaries of the game. Thereafter, each player attempts to capture any of his opponents' marbles, in turn, by tossing his marble such that it lodges within his five finger hand span from a specific opponent's marble. If successful, he captures that marble and collects any side bet (usually a quantity of other marbles) made before play began. He may otherwise opt to make a defensive toss so as to reposition his marble to a more advantageous location. A toss or throw which directly contacts the attacked marble, regardless of where the tossed marble comes to rest, also captures the marble struck. Play continues until all but one marble is captured.

One of several versions of baseball adapted to alleyways and narrow vacant lots was an apparently unique activity called Triggy. The only equipment required to play this game is a broom handle from which two sections are cut. One, a short piece four to five inches long, half of which is whittled to form a tapered blunt point, becomes the triggy. The other piece of broomstick is left with squared ends and measures about 18 inches in length. This is identified as the triggy stick. Also, it may be necessary to find a small flat stone to use as a launching pad for the triggy.

Looking in a dictionary, I found that a trig is the name given to a wedge or block employed to prevent a wheel or cask from rolling. One can infer the connection. A triggy when launched is not apt to do a lot of rolling.

Now we have, except for the playing field, all that is needed to play the game.

After choosing two teams, each with any number from three upward, one team takes the field. An alley, parking lot, a low traffic street will do. The other team will be "up" (meaning at bat). The batter (I don't recall if that was the term used) places the triggy on the small flat stone, unless the playing field conveniently provides a curbstone or similarly raised surface, such that the tapered end is pointed toward the field and overhangs the stone at a slight upward angle to the ground or pavement. With the triggy stick, the batter taps the overhanging end of the triggy with a downward stroke whereby the triggy flips upward to about waist height spinning end over end. As it nears its apogee, he strikes the triggy toward the field with a swing of the triggy stick. (Glass windows in the vicinity could suddenly become causes for immediate postponement.)

If any fielder on the opposing team catches the triggy in mid-air before it touches the ground regardless of the triggy's rebounding or ricocheting off of a structure bounding or standing in the field, the batter is out. If any fielder can catch the triggy after it bounces on the ground once, he is entitled to two throws at the triggy stick (explanation follows). Should a fielder catch the triggy after more than one bounce or retrieve it when it comes to rest, he will get only one throw at the triggy stick.

The batter, after striking the triggy, places the triggy stick vertically on the ground near where the triggy was struck, holding the stick in an upright stance with his index finger. The stick is thus the target for the throw (or throws) of the fielder who retrieved the triggy. The fielder throws the triggy at the triggy stick from the place where he retrieved the triggy, the object being to land the triggy as close as he can to the triggy stick or to hit it directly, in which case the batter will be out. If the fielder is allowed two throws, the second throw follows the first from the point at which it came to rest, much like putting in golf.

When the triggy comes to rest, at whatever distance from the triggy stick, after the throw(s) without contacting the stick, the batter estimates the number of stick lengths in a straight line to where the triggy lies and calls out a number he thinks will fall short of the number estimated by as close as he dares, for the greater the number, the more points that are scored. The batter is then obliged to walk the stick end over end directly toward the triggy, counting as he goes and scores the number he has called. Should the number of stick lengths to the triggy be less than the number called, the batter is declared out and does not score.

214

As in baseball, players bat in rotation and three outs are allowed per side up. The winning point score can be established as a finite number achieved by the team reaching that number first, or again like baseball, by playing a set number of innings with the highest score winning.

This recalls many of the street games by which we as children amused ourselves during the years between the two great wars. We played with the resources available and affordable. We were a happy lot and rarely got into serious trouble. It was a different time.

Additional Reading:
Grover, Kathryn, ed. *Hard at Play: Leisure in America 1840-1940*. Amherst: University of Massachusetts Press, 1992.

Grunfeld, Frederic V., ed. *Games of the World: How to Make Them..How to Play Them..How They Came to Be*. New York: Holt, Rhinehart and Winston, 1975.

Opie, Iona and Peter. *Children's Games in Street and Playground*. London: Oxford University Press, 1969.

Marvin Engel, born in 1924, was raised and schooled in and around Albany, New York, interrupted by three years in the U.S. Army during World War II. He received degrees in Engineering and in Applied Mechanics from the Rennselaer Polytechnic Institute. Shortly thereafter, he and his family made a job related move to the Philadelphia area. The design, construction and testing of complex mechanical devices summarizes his principal occupational involvements. Writing technical reports and scientific papers, followed in several instances by their presentation and journal publication, were much a part of these activities throughout his professional career. After retiring in 1989 , Marvin has been residing in the Woodlands, Texas (near Houston); however, he revisits his northeastern roots for an extended period each year.

YOLANDE A. GOTTLIEB

Maria Estela Nemesia Nibot Mena de Nieto Story

Catapulted Through Life

Grandma Estela, who was born in 1892, became pensive for a few minutes and then sank back on her comfortable leather recliner.

"Yes, dear, I do remember a lot about the Depression years - we spent some of them here in the United States, and some of them in Europe - and no, we didn't suffer too much. I guess we were some of the fortunate ones. We had many close calls and there were some very frightening moments. You might even say we had quite a few adventures - but we never went without food or shelter. The Lord was very good to us.

"Your grandfather Ismael and I came to the United States in 1923, years before the big Crash. Ironically one of the reasons we left Havana was because of what he felt to be dire instability; Cuba was a country where government was a joke, where it seemed every president sought to make a fortune, where the economy swayed like rennet.

"Many powerful families we knew lost everything; empires crumbled. He realized being in the upper crust was not a sure thing with such a shaky foundation.

"He wanted better for us and our four children. We needed long term stability. Your grandpa was an idealist. He had been to high school in the United States and had gone to the University of Havana to become an accountant. Through the years he traveled to this country very often; he loved it. He loved everything about it; this was paradise to him. The people were wonderful, there was no crooked government here, the economy was sound, the system was perfect. This was the land of opportunity and my husband was a hard worker with big dreams.

"Besides, something happened that helped him make the final decision. His family owned a thriving accounting business in Havana, and he was one of the four owners. He worked with

217

them full-time for many years, but his father, who was a very domineering man, saw business procedures in a different way than the children did. Ismael opted for letting him have his way. He kept his interest in the business, but accepted an offer for a job with the "Ferrocarriles Unidos" (United Railroad Systems.) He became an accountant in the administration building. Your grandfather was a very bright young man with an excellent business mind. He started solving a lot of problems that the business office had found insurmountable. Within a year he was offered the position of Director of Business Affairs, which he accepted. This caused a lot of commotion within the company because there were senior employees who were in line for that position. As time went by, two of them made Ismael's life so miserable that he decided it was not worth the aggravation and resigned. We sold our beautiful home, some property, and everything else we owned and moved to Tampa, Florida.

"Part of the money was invested in opening a restaurant which your grandfather managed. The restaurant was so successful that he kept on expanding and hiring more and more people to run it. Eventually he decided to ask his younger brother Edward to come and help run the restaurant because he needed someone he could trust.

"Now, Edward was the black sheep of the family. He had done some dishonest things in his youth much to the chagrin of the entire family - but your grandfather trusted him and loved him blindly.

"Within a few years Edward had built himself a home, brought his wife and children to Tampa, and before we knew it, we had lost the restaurant to him. Heartbroken and disgusted, my sweet husband sold our home in Tampa and moved all of us to an apartment in New York City.

"Life wasn't easy, much to Ismael's dismay. That unshakable American economy had hit bottom and we were caught in it. Fortunately we still had some money in the bank to weather the storm.

"Your grandpa knew a lot about photography and film making. He had learned most of it from an uncle who owned a film company and some movie houses in Havana. When he was a student and needed extra money, he would take to the country with his camera and photograph farmers, children, and so forth.

218

Or else, if he had the opportunity, he would do some film editing at his uncle's company. He always had money....

"That experience came in very handy during the Depression. He bought a camera and dark room equipment, which he set up in a closet and in the bathroom of our apartment. The next morning off he went to near-by towns and photographed children on farms, on the streets, at stores, and in any and every place he could find. He'd give the parents a card with a number, and set up appointments to bring the pictures to their home a few days later.

"We had negatives and photos hanging from lines all over the apartment!

"He kept looking for a permanent job, but there were no jobs available. Grandpa was earning a fair income with his camera, but there was little extra. We were struggling and had to buy necessities for the children; you know how it is, they grow out of shoes and clothes constantly. Besides, we now had four seasons to contend with, they all needed winter coats and snow boots.

"I was very frugal all my life and more so during those Depression years. Why, I remember taking the collars and cuffs off your grandpa's shirts when they started to fray, turning them inside out and sewing them back on, so they looked new again. Of course clothes used to last much longer then - I think the materials were better. Back then shirts were washed, rinsed with bluing and starched with liquid starch. (It is so easy now with spray starch!) We ironed shirts while they were still damp. They came out looking like you had just bought them at the store!

"You talk of recycling now - women in those days used to make skirts from old men's slacks, make children's shorts and little dresses from sheets, pillow cases, old skirts, anything. We saved every scrap of material for tablecloths, throw pillows, and of course quilts. We even replaced the soles of socks when they wore out! I don't know how we had time for everything, but we did. I embroidered all the girls' clothing. My children were always neatly dressed and sparkling clean - I taught them well!

"I felt I should help and took in 'home work' - I made lampshades for a company that had advertised in the newspapers. They paid me seventy-five cents for each finished product. There was a lot of work involved in dressing a lampshade, but the children helped cut the strips of cloth, thread needles, and sort the trimmings, making the task much easier.

"The second time I (and my four little ones) delivered the shades to the company, the manager in charge of the 'home work' realized my situation. He suggested that from then on, someone from his office would bring the materials to my apartment and pick up the finished product so I would not have to leave home. He was a very nice and considerate man.

"Ismael had convinced me that America was, indeed, the land of opportunity. He believed that this was only a temporary setback and I trusted his judgment. I knew we would triumph over any vicissitudes.

"One day he came home very excited - he had met Eli Levy in the subway. Eli was an old friend whom he had not seen in many years and who was working for Warner Brothers at the time. He told Ismael that finding him was short of a miracle - he desperately needed someone who knew motion pictures and spoke several languages. Grandpa fit the bill. He started working the following week.

"This was in 1930. Grandfather worked for Warner Brothers as a film editor. His job, besides editing and adding subtitles to films that were to be shown in foreign countries, entailed verifying that all the translations from English to French, Italian, Portuguese and Spanish were perfectly correct for each of the different countries where the films would be shown.

"It was of utmost importance not to allow any idiomatic expressions that were incorrect to slip by. Surprising as it was, a common word in two countries, or even two regions of the same country that spoke the same language, could be an offensive word in one and a perfectly correct word in another. This was the case among many of the Spanish speaking countries, but a common occurrence in other languages as well.

"It appeared that our struggling days were over. Ismael loved his job and was secure in his position. We continued to be very conservative and tried to save every cent we could; the Depression was still hurting a lot of people.

"One of my friends lost her husband; she was left penniless with a car and a six-year-old child. She packed their things in the car and went through the city looking for a large empty house. She asked a landlord if he minded her taking in boarders, and if he would take a chance on her. She would pay him by the week as the money came in. He even lent her some money so she could turn the place into a boarding house. She then went to the grocery store and asked for credit, promising to pay back by the week. The man agreed and she set out to work. My friend and her six-year-old worked their fingers to the bone. That poor child helped her in the kitchen, helped make beds, dusted and polished until he was too tired to move. She worked all day and late into the night; then early up again to prepare meals. She almost worked herself to an early grave, but she paid back the money and eventually saved enough to buy a house where she rented rooms. Those Depression years tore many people down, but for some it was a true test of courage!

"In 1933, a few months before Christmas, Alfredo Castelvil, an old friend of the family, traveled to New York hoping to convince Grandfather to go back to Spain with him. He was setting up a three-way partnership in a big motion picture company venture. He wanted Ismael to be the third partner and film director.

"After much deliberation the proposition was accepted - we would invest in the film company. Preparations began to relocate the family to Spain.

"By then Carmen, your mother, who had just turned twenty, Oscar who was barely seventeen, Olga fifteen, and Hilda fourteen, were all excited about the move and looked forward to discovery and adventure in a foreign country. Besides they were going to meet all the movie stars!

"We boarded the cargo ship 'Motomar' which was the only one going to Spain immediately. The voyage lasted twenty-eight days. We had perfect weather. The children had a marvelous time; the radio operator took them under his wing and spoiled them to no end. By the time we landed he had shown them every nook and cranny of the ship. He'd round up members of the crew and they'd play games every afternoon.

"It was all fun with the exception of the time the first mate took your mother's shoe off when she was sitting on deck and started tossing it back and forth to the radio operator and another crew member while she tried to take it away from them - the first mate missed and the shoe went overboard.... It was your mom's favorite pair of navy blue shoes, and I don't think she ever forgave them.

221

"In the evenings they'd play music and show us different regional dances. They even made up a play, which was a satire based on the Spanish Monarchy, that kept us in stitches.

"The cook made special regional Spanish meals for our sake (an attempt to indoctrinate us on the marvelous variety of their country's cuisine). This was far better than any luxury liner could have been. We loved it.

"As we came into port in Barcelona, early morning, the first thing we saw was a very large statue of Christopher Colombus, a similar sight to the Statue of Liberty in New York.

"Castelvil and the other partner, Carlos Padron, were waiting for us at the pier. They took us to a temporary furnished apartment in downtown Barcelona that their secretary had found for us. Then on to lunch and their studio.

"The studio was in a large warehouse-type building. It had a very plush office with thick oriental carpets and heavy, carved mahogany furniture. There were champagne, petit fours, and a beautiful assortment of chocolates on a large marble-top table. Six members of the staff who manned the office joined the group to welcome us. We were treated like royalty; it was very fashionable then to come from America....Besides, there were 'classes' in Spain at that time; you were either rich or poor - and we were 'the rich.' It was nice to be upper class again - during the Depression in the States we had been part of the struggling middle class who became poor very fast.

"At any rate, after the introductions and welcoming, your grandfather stayed to get acquainted with the office, and the children and I were sent home in Castelvil's chauffeured car.

"We were all too tired to do anything more - the apartment was cold, we couldn't find any trace of heaters anywhere. That night we all went to sleep in our winter coats. The next day the apartment was a bit warmer but it started getting real cold in the afternoon. I found the apartment 'portera' (manager) and asked her how we heated the place. She explained that we had to buy coal and use the brazier which was in the living room. We had not seen any such thing and she came to show us. There was a large table in the middle of the room which had a tablecloth on it, (we had assumed it was a coffee table). She removed the tablecloth, lifted the wood cover and pointed to a container with a very large bowl, which was to be used for burning coal. We were supposed to sit around the table and warm our feet by placing them near the heat source. 'But this,' she said, 'will only be necessary when it gets cold, these are very mild days.' We asked what happened when we needed to go to sleep. She said, 'Hot water bottles of course.'

"We were freezing. It was a damp type of cold that went right through to our bones, and there was no getting away from it; every place we went was just as cold. There was no way to warm up, so that night we put on three and four layers of clothing, piled socks on socks, gathered blankets and went to our freezing beds.

"We were used to the efficient heating in New York City, where apartment buildings had heat piped through and by 6:00 a.m. the apartment was warm. All you ever had to do, if the apartment was cold when you got up, was to go to the building's janitor and ask for the heat to be turned on high. (Although that rarely happened, as someone usually banged on the pipes if that was the case.)

"Here we were newly arrived in Barcelona in a very cold apartment and with only a brazier. I went and bought coal for it and we started a fire, then went about getting settled. One by one the children said they weren't feeling well and went to bed. I didn't think much about it, because we were all so tired, and I don't know when I passed out, but when Ismael brought me back, the brazier was out, all the windows and doors were open and the children were all back to normal. Padrón, who had come home with Ismael to visit us, had sized up the situation immediately and acted on it - he saved our lives.

"It was explained to me that I had bought the wrong kind of coal and it had toxic fumes! It was a real education. Needless to say, the house we would move to had to have normal heating.

"By the next morning we had had it; I was afraid the children were going to get pneumonia and die. Ismael had asked Castelvil to help him find a house with good heating, and he did.

"The motion picture business was very successful. The children did get to meet many movie stars. Your grandfather would appear at the house with different movie stars and stars-to-be all the time.

"By the way, that is how your mother met your dad - he wanted to be in the movies. He came from a very good family in

Barcelona. He had been an 'Alferez de Fragata' (Ensign) in the Spanish Royal Navy and was a medical student with aspirations to stardom when they met. The courtship lasted about a year; they married in the Catholic Church and set up a very fancy apartment near us.

"But let me go back to 1933. We stayed at the temporary apartment a few days, then moved to a house on a street called 'Villaroel.' It was a lovely house with marble floors and very tall ceilings. There was beautiful Spanish tile work throughout the entire house and windows that went from floor to ceiling. I especially remember the front door. It was gigantic and beautifully carved dark wood, but it was far too heavy; it made a hollow sound that rang through the entire house when it closed. This was more like our home in Havana, but I don't think it ever felt 'cozy' to us.

"The children went to school and found that they were taught mostly in Catalonian (the local dialect of the region) and then in Castilian, both of which they had to learn, but with the help of some tutors they adapted readily.

"Vacations were spent in the mountains - they had beautiful resorts and most of the time the Castelvil family and the Padrón family spent holidays at the same places we did. We grew very fond of each other and had marvelous times together.

"Life was pleasant in Barcelona and things were going well for our family. Oscar, our only boy, started working as a cameraman for the company and spent a lot of time with his father. Your mother was married and moved to Menorca, where your father was sent after being drafted by the military. You were on the way.

"Olga, our most adventurous daughter, had decided to become a movie star, and when dad said 'NO!' she set out to prove she ruled herself by secretly entering a beauty contest which she won, much to your grandpa's consternation.

"Hilda brought a touch of sunshine to our lives with her happy disposition. How many times I thanked the Lord for her constant smiles - even through the coming years, when we were caught in the turmoil of the civil war, she was always filled with hope; always smiling.

"You were born in Menorca in 1935, and your parents moved back to Barcelona to the apartment they had left, which had been in the care of your father's family.

"There was an underlying current of unrest in the country since the Republic was proclaimed in 1931, and culminated in 1936 in the 'Guerra de Liberación' (Liberation War) which translated into the Spanish civil war, and lasted until 1939 - but I don't want to go into the political aspects of that war. A good history book will tell you more than I ever could.

"The country was divided into two factions: the Republicans and the Military (which eventually became the 'Franquistas'). The populace took to the streets. They looted and burned grocery stores making food scarce, and ransacked other establishments. Men and women armed themselves with rifles, bayonets, knives and clubs to hand out their personal choice of justice. If someone didn't like you they would denounce you to one of the factions and you would get shot, no questions asked.

"The Republicans would ride in cars and trucks and would stop you on the street and ask you to give 'the signal.' You were supposed to raise your right hand in a tight fist to signify you were a Republican. If you gave the wrong signal they shot you on the spot. At night we would hear trucks coming to unload prisoners. They would line them up against the wall of a building across the street from where we lived and shoot them. It was a nightmare! There were nights when this would go on and on; you would hear people pleading for mercy and getting shot down.

"An official letter came for your father with orders to go to Pamplona to re-unite with his battalion. Your mother told him that she could not stay in the country because the food shortage affected you. You were about a year old then. If he went to fight and she had to leave Barcelona they might never find each other again. But she had found a way of getting him out of the country and into Italy where they could wait until things settled down. Then they could return to Spain. He told her that would make him a deserter and he could not do that; he had to fight for his country no matter what happened.

"Meanwhile, as destiny would have it, the transport that was supposed to pick him up was blown up by the Republicans and everyone in it was killed, many of his friends included. He had to wait for another transport to reach Barcelona and by then your mother had convinced him to leave. One night, breaking curfew, the two of them stole away through the darkened streets

225

to the home of some Cuban friends who had the Cuban flag flying in front of their home. Your father remained with them, hiding. Neither the Republicans nor the Franquistas would bother those who flew other countries' flags; they had immunity.

"As we feared, one day some Republicans came to search our house, probably looking for your father. I greeted them at the door, calm and collected, and asked them to come in to have a cup of coffee. Once they were in the kitchen I asked why they were breaking their rules and checking a home which was flying a Cuban flag. They were common people and felt intimidated by me, for which I was very grateful. They hemmed and hawed for a few minutes and then excused themselves and left. After I closed the door behind them I shook like a leaf. You see, one of your father's uniforms was hanging behind my bedroom door. The laundry woman had found no one at their apartment and had left it with me the day before. Of course, if they had found the uniform they would have shot us for being Franquistas.

"Your grandfather and Uncle Oscar were hired by the Ministry of War and were sent to the front to take motion pictures of the war. I was terrified, I feared for their lives.

"In an attempt to leave Barcelona before your father was found, your mother and three of the Cuban Ambassador's children, who had gone to school with Oscar, went to the Cuban Embassy. They had offered to help us. While one of the boys distracted his father, the other two helped your mother switch the pictures in Oscar's passport for your father's picture. They carefully matched the official embassy seal on your father's picture and positioned it back on the page where Oscar's picture had been. Then they waited for the visa to be granted. When the Ambassador interviewed your mother, she had to pose as being an unwed mother having to confess her predicament to him. She told him she was fleeing the country with her brother and baby because there was no available food. It was very embarrassing, and the well-meaning Ambassador felt obligated to give her a sermon on the precariousness of sin. Besides, she had to keep a straight face while the boys had fun mocking the situation behind their father's chair. The following week your mom, dad and you boarded the ship 'Principessa Giovanni' via Genoa, and I didn't see you for what seemed an eternity.

"Many months later, since we had heard nothing from

226

Ismael or Oscar, I asked the Cuban Ambassador to intercede and see if he could find out where they were. He brought us dismal news, they were lost; assumed dead. Grief stricken, I made arrangements to leave Barcelona with Olga and Hilda and travel to Havana, where I still had family.

"We left the same way your parents had, with thirty duros (about twenty dollars) and one valise. (That was all you were allowed to take out of the country.) An Italian ship took us to Genoa where we stayed for many months while waiting for Cuba to decide to claim us.

"The Cuban government did not want to accept responsibility for any more refugees who had fled from Spain. Mussolini got tired of arguing with them and sent an official proclamation. In it he stated how he deplored their lack of loyalty to their subjects, and their general attitude. Then he added that Italy would be more than happy to accept all the refugees, but that they treated their people very well and they would have to bill the Cuban government for all expenses. Within two-and-half weeks we were boarding the ship 'El Recca' via Cuba.

"We arrived in Havana, and, much to my relief, your mother and father were there as well. One night we were all sitting together and exchanging stories of our exodus. Carmen told us that when they had boarded the ship the captain suddenly ordered to have the plank lifted and asked everyone to line up on deck. Your mother passed by one of the ship mates who had been playing with you earlier, and she asked him what was happening. He whispered, 'There are two spies with false documents on board... we have to find them.' The shock made her almost drop you to the floor, but your father caught you and pushed you back up in her arms. She took a few hesitant steps and said, 'What do we do now?' Your father took you in his arms and answered, 'Nothing, we do nothing.' After what seemed an eternity the plank was lowered again and boarding was resumed. Carmen asked the same ship mate what had happened, he said, 'Oh it was the two Germans with the little dog, they had false papers but they have been taken off board and will be shot. You need not fear.'

"The Principessa Giovanni was used as a hospital ship to bring wounded Italian soldiers from Ethiopia. There were not enough quarters for all the refugees, and most of the mattresses

227

were covered with dried blood from wounded soldiers, some had small pieces of decayed flesh. Your mother pleaded with the ship mate to see if he could find a clean place where she could put you down to sleep. He promised to help and brought back a mattress which was fairly clean on one side. He said it was his mattress, and he put it under a piano in the bar. 'Here,' he said, 'you sleep here with the baby.' There is much more to tell you, you should ask your mother to give you more details sometime....

"Ismael and Oscar finally appeared in Havana a year-and-a-half later, safe and sound.

"Your grandfather and I came back to New York after that. He went back to work for Warner Brothers, and we lived well and happily until he died in 1967.

"By the time we returned to New York the big Depression was almost over. However, I honestly feel that even though those were the terrible Thirties, we are in a worse depression now than we were back then.

"I was fortunate that my son was a bit too old to go to World War II.

"After Ismael died I moved in with your mother who had been divorced a few years, but that is a story for another time.

"I am ninety-nine you know, I wonder if anyone realizes that I have seen it all...."

I remember when I was little and Grandma Estela put me to sleep by singing lullabies and scratching my back, and how she always held a captive audience of grandchildren at story-telling time.

I got up from the sofa and went to give her a hug and a kiss.

"Oh Grandma," I said, "I can't wait until December when you turn one hundred; we are already planning your birthday party!" She giggled as she returned the kiss.

Grandma, Maria Estela Nemesia Nibot Mena de Nieto as her full name went, left our side on April 12, 1996; she was 104. Grandma had a gentle passing, but not before crowning her years with yet another milestone; she became an American citizen the day she turned one hundred years old. What a wonderful example she has left for us to emulate!

Yolande A. Gottlieb was born in Menorca, Spain, lived between Cuba and the United States for most of her youth. She is married and has three boys, one girl, five grandchildren, a twenty-five year old parrot, a dog, an Australian Pigmy hedgehog, and an aquarium full of fish she has named. Yolande is a published poet and writer, founder of an in-depth study group called Poets at Work, Counselor for the Poetry Society of Texas. She was Juried Poet at the 1994 Houston Poetry Fest and recipient of the Houston Literary Arts Award in 1996. She is owner and publisher of Poet's Journey, i.e. magazine and Astra Press.

GUIDA JACKSON

Guida Jackson is an observer who writes and teaches in the Woodlands, Texas, where she lives with her artist husband and their two labs amid a huge untidy pile of books. She holds a BA in Journalism, MA in Third World Literature, and PhD in Comparative Literature, and is the author of several books and plays. Since 1976 she has been managing editor of *Touchstone Literary Journal*.

JACKIE PELHAM

Jackie Pelham is a writer and publisher who holds a BA in Creative Writing. She has published at the local, state and national levels which includes poetry, short stories, feature stories, a children's book and a cookbook. She lives in North Houston with her husband and is dedicated to documenting the literature of Texas.

Much appreciation is owed to William H. Laufer who proofread the editors' proofreading.